All together you

THIS BOOK BELONGS TO:

Emma Chiappetta

NAME

27 DARLINGTON CRES. - BRAMPTON

ADDRESS

905- 791-1221

PHONE

All together you

SECOND EDITION

By Bette DeHaven

with Ruth Milliron

© 1991, 1995 InterNET Services Corporation and Bette DeHaven
All Rights Reserved. Duplication Prohibited.
Printed in the USA
ISBN 0-932877-46-X
BK347

Second Edition: 1st printing December 1995

Printed on recycled paper.

CONTENTS

ACKNOWLEDGEMENTS

This book is definitely a combined effort. So many wonderful people have helped make it possible. Ruth Milliron, my sister, collaborated and critiqued the entire effort. She deserves the entire credit for Chapter 7, "Am I Ready To Go Shopping?" Her God-given talent in the area of fashion coordination has been a great inspiration to me. My husband's patience and help were so necessary. My associate, Sue Cappelen, was and is such an encouragement to me.

The creativity and ideas of Penny Onley and Joann Bellavia at Designwise along with the editing expertise of Valerie Munei at InterNET were invaluable in producing this book. The illustrations, done by Betty Ruhl, made it all come alive. The glass frame expertise I owe to Georgeanne Kahn, owner of The Optical Shop in Toledo, Ohio. I appreciate the faith the Yagers have in me; it made this book possible.

Last, but certainly not least, I thank my heavenly Father for giving me the desire, the persistence and the people mentioned above to bring this book to completion.

Thank you each and every one!

—Bette DeHaven

ABOUT THE AUTHORS...

Bette DeHaven, owner of the California-based company **Designer's Touch,** has over 21 years of experience in all areas of the color and image industry.

Bette obtained her formal education in clothing and textiles from Ohio Wesleyan University and East Texas State University. She also minored in art and design.

Through the years Bette has given thousands of private consultations and presented programs to various professional groups and institutions, such as banks, colleges, law firms, churches, and plastic surgeons. In addition to her continuous performance in these areas, she has developed and directs seminars for **The Crowning Touch**™ and **Expressions In Color,** national image organizations.

BETTE DEHAVEN

Ruth Milliron is the owner of **Embellir Custom Cosmetics and Salons.** She is also author of *Spring and Fall Fashion Perspectives,* seasonal style catalogs. For the past 19 years, Ruth, a Certified Color and Image Consultant, has instructed numerous clients in all areas of image development. Ruth also consults on an individual basis, creates seasonal style shows, and lectures nationally.

She received her bachelor of science degree in clothing textiles and design from Bowling Green State University, where she has served as an administrator for 20 years.

RUTH MILLIRON

INTRODUCTION

Personal style is something everyone has, but not everyone is sure how best to express it. You may already know what yours is, but perhaps you haven't been able to pull it together into a total look.

Personal style is an outward expression of an inner attitude about ourselves. It is the totality of our look—from hairstyle to shoes. It is evidenced by how we put our clothes together on our figure and finish it off with accessories. Someone with good personal style understands her colors, what lines and designs flatter her body, and how to express her personality through her clothing choices. She has cultivated and developed good taste, and she puts it all together with harmony and consistency. She is a woman who always looks good, whether you see her at a party, run into her at the supermarket, meet with her on the job, or happen to catch her in her bathrobe. Personal style is a lifelong process. Each of us is at a different point in the process. So don't stop reading because you are afraid this is too ambitious an undertaking.

If you have a laid-back attitude, you will need to apply a greater effort in this venture than someone who has either an adventuresome spirit or a more perfectionist type of temperament. The following guidelines should help you:

- Develop a new awareness of what "put together" women are doing.

- Seek professional advice on your wardrobe building.

- Observe the principles professionals use as they work with you.

- Remember successful people are not intimidated by what they don't know.

- You can learn!

The following features are also important components of good personal style:

- Wearing colors that compliment the natural hair, skin, and eye colors.

- Choosing hair color that is correct for your skin tone.

- Applying cosmetics that compliment the skin tone and enhance the eyes.

- Selecting clothing lines that compliment the figure frame and disguise any figure flaws.

- Choosing clothing that says, "This is who I am at my best!"

- Selecting accessories that harmonize with the lines and personality of the garment worn.

- Wearing fabrics that are compatible with each other.

- Dressing consistently with your personality and lifestyle; wearing the greatest look for whatever activity you are involved in.

- Keeping current with your look.

- Maintaining a rich or quality look. (It does not have to be expensive.)

To further clarify, I would like to add a list of less tangible qualities. These would describe the attitude of a woman who has achieved good personal style.

- Ageless. She decides she will never become dowdy or matronly.

- Mysterious. She has a certain element of fascination, not revealing all about herself.

- Sophisticated. She is wise in the ways of the world but doesn't follow them unless it's appropriate to do so.

- Confident. She is comfortable with her body and look, thus enabling her to concentrate on others without a nagging concern for how others see her.

HOW TO USE THIS BOOK

This book will provide you with some excellent guidelines and principles in developing your image. It includes everything from the foundation of color to ways to compliment your total look and uniqueness of style.

Personal style rarely comes effortlessly or even naturally. Many of us, from a very young age, know what type of clothing we like, whether it is sporty or romantic, etc. The development of these preferences into good personal style takes a knowledge of what looks good and how to put it together successfully. Personal style is an invention or a creation born to each individual woman. Therefore, good taste and judgement must be learned and developed, and then exercised in choosing fashions that best express who you are.

There are some dangers we encounter when we shop for ourselves. One is the attempt to imitate someone else's look or style. Because no two people are exactly alike, unless you are an identical twin, you can never look the way that person does in her clothes and accessories. Role models are important but not for carbon copying because you will usually look like a counterfeit!

Have you ever tried on an outfit exactly the way it was displayed? Were you disappointed with the way it looked on you? That is because the outfit was not chosen for you. In fact, some things only look good on display!

Another pitfall to good style is in trying to overcome negative feedback received in past years, particularly the teenage years. In many instances, you forsake who you really are to become something or someone you are not.

In this book, we will consider the following components of good personal style:

- Your physical characteristics (coloring, hair type, body frame, and body proportions).

- Your clothing personality (your personal style and personality traits).

- Your wardrobe-planning skills and shopping habits.

I have worked in the image field for years. What I share in the following pages is a result of what I have observed and learned about women's needs and how to best meet those needs while building a positive and successful image, both inside and out. Just remember, successful people are not intimidated by what they don't know. They act on what knowledge they already have and are always looking for growth opportunities. A successful image develops with a woman's growth and continues to develop throughout her life.

NOTES

the
crowning
touch ™

THE CROWNING TOUCH™ SEMINARS

To gain hands-on experience with the principles of this book that will develop your self-confidence and the skills to help others discover their own personal styles, the following seminars are also available to you.

INTRODUCTION TO COOL/WARM COLOR ANALYSIS, ARTISTRY®/NUTRILITE®, AND PERSONAL IMAGE DEVELOPMENT

This seminar will motivate and teach distributors how to use Artistry® cosmetics through cool/warm color analysis and beginning image principles.

ADVANCED COLOR CERTIFICATION

This specialized course trains women in full seasonal color analysis, make-up application, and marketing.

ADVANCED IMAGE AND SHOPPING

This course will provide *advanced* personal knowledge in image, wardrobing, and shopping techniques.

If you would like more information on color and personal image seminars contact either:

■
Bette DeHaven
c/o The Crowning Touch™/Designer's Touch
18030 Brookhurst #335
Fountain Valley, CA 92708

■
The Crowning Touch™
P.O. Box 412080
Charlotte, NC 28241-8834

CHAPTER ONE

ARE MY COLORS SHOWING?

The foundation for good image is color.

It affects your self-perception or the way you see yourself. It definitely affects how others see and respond to you. Because color either creates an attractive, healthy, and rested appearance on the face or the exact opposite, we should certainly desire the former result.

Secondly, color should not be the first thing people see when we enter a room. If it is, then the color is wearing us. For the most effective image, color must enhance and be in balance with our natural coloring. When we realize that color has tremendous power to influence others, we will undoubtedly want to choose personal colors that promote a positive image and at the same time successfully influence our purpose in a business or social situation.

Color psychologists and researchers have published some very valuable information for anyone interested. Every color affects us either psychologically or physiologically. Many of our responses are totally involuntary. For example, navy blue, which became the professional uniform in the 1980s, speaks of intellect and gives a message of credibility and authority. When combined with yellow, communication usually becomes more open because yellow is called the "nonverbal mouth." So we could say that with the use of a navy blue suit and a yellow accent, we could gain immediate credibility and authority while appearing to be a good communicator. This is all accomplished in a matter of seconds with no verbal communication.

Most of us have heard we only have one chance to make a good first impression. If you react to that statement by saying it is unfair, you are right, but unfortunately most men and women are unable to get beyond the outward appearance and see the heart of others most of the time. We make judgments about people regarding their social status, income, level of education, or sophistication in a matter of minutes without even realizing it.

People are not necessarily drawn to colors that compliment them. Because we are emotional beings, we respond to color both physiologically and psychologically. So our experiences greatly influence our choices. I do find that more women prefer cooler colors than warm and that more men prefer warm colors than cool until such time as their education and experience is broadened. Individuals who do not have good self-esteem will shy away from bold blue-based colors unless they have been conditioned as a child to be positive toward these colors. Obviously then, we cannot depend upon our emotions in this realm, but we must be open to good, objective advice.

My approach to color analysis is based on the Season Theory because it provides an easy-to-understand, effective way to develop a disciplined wardrobe. When the characteristics of each of the seasonal palettes are explained to have a direct relationship to the seasons of the year, people can visualize the qualities of these color palettes more readily. Over the years, this technique has been used by several image companies, and each has adapted it to their particular philosophy. I have come to believe that the four-season approach needs to have its application expanded. The greatest need comes between Winter and Summer. This palette is called Winter II. It accommodates the softer Winter and the darker Summer characteristics that will be discussed further on in this chapter.

SEASONS OF COLOR

WINTER

Winter hues are pure, clean, bold, and sharply contrasting. They are true primary or blue-based in undertone. Just visualize clean, new fallen snow resting on wet, dark tree bark and pine needles, then contrast this against the crisp, deep blue sky of a winter day—then you have the essence of the Winter color palette.

The Winter's look is of the highest of contrasts or of rich deep coloring. She wears clear *primary* colors or high-contrast colors best. If her eyes are dark brown with medium brown hair color, then Winter I palette is best. The dark eyes overrule the lighter hair.

WINTER II

The Winter II hues are saturated—medium to dark, some smoky and some brighter. Yellow and maize are the only lighter hues. The Winter II person looks most outstanding in shades of medium blue-green to hunter, turquoise, raspberry to burgundy, bright to deep and smoky purples, and periwinkle to shades of navy. The neutral family best for this person is taupe to charcoal brown. She does not wear black. It can only be used as an accent color when incorporated into the garment or print in a minimal degree. Several of the colors found here are in Winter and Summer swatch books available on the color tool market. Several are unique to the Winter II palette.

The overall look is softer than Winter I. This person usually does not tan quickly and may burn first. The palette includes deeper, more intense colors, primarily the saturated jewel tones.

SUMMER

Summer hues are soft, dusty, and grayed. They have a blue-based undertone. Now visualize a summer day. The sun shines more directly overhead causing the colors to become softer, especially if the humidity levels are high. A misty quality takes over the color of the sky and landscape. When you think of flowers like sweet peas, snapdragons, stock, etc., you can see the qualities of Summer pinks, lavenders, white, etc.

This person has a look of softness with a low contrast between skin and hair color. She looks best when dressed in cool, subtle colors either in combination or monochromatically. She should avoid strong, vivid colors that can overpower her.

SPRING

Spring hues are clean, clear, and somewhat delicate in quality but with a yellow base or undertone. Freshness and clarity are the qualities of color this time of year. As you visualize springtime, all color—whether green, red, yellow, or blue—seems to be warmed by the bright sunlight. It's especially easy to visualize the budding of new life in the springtime with its yellow-green quality.

The Spring person does not have high contrast between skin and hair color. Therefore, she should avoid muddy or dark colors, blue reds or blue pinks, dark browns, and of course, black and pure white.

AUTUMN

Autumn hues are warm, rich, earthy, and mellow with a golden undertone in the yellow-base side of color. Picture breathtaking New England trees in all their golden, orange, and red hues. As the sun sets, the landscape glows with an intense warmth.

This person can wear the rich earth tones with a golden undertone. She wears the greens extremely well from muddied olive to rich forest green. In addition to the earthy colors, many Autumns need or can wear some bright colors closely related to Spring. If she is naturally black-haired, she can sometimes add black to her wardrobe.

CHARACTERISTICS OF EACH SEASON

Typical physical features.

SEASONS OF COLOR

WINTER	WINTER II
skin tones—cool or blue undertone:	**skin tones—cool or blue undertone:**
Fair or porcelain	Porcelain (fair)
Pink or rose beige	Rose beige (could have brown freckling)
Light olive, olive to black (often lacks cheek color)	Ruddy (uneven complexion)
Ruddy with red or pink uneven complexion	Sallow beige (surface color)
hair color:	**hair color:**
Black—blue-black or black with brown	Medium brown to ash (gray) brown
Dark brown	Chestnut brown
Dark brown with burgundy highlights	Burgundy brown
Silver gray	Silver gray
White	
Salt and pepper (black with gray or white)	
Note: Winters should always color gray hair with a solid, natural tone if hair coloring is desired.	
eye color:	**eye color:**
Black brown	Blue or aqua
Light to dark brown	Blue gray or soft gray
Blue, gray blue, or blue-violet	Green, gray green
Green, gray green, olive green/brown, or hazel	Hazel
Note: Yellow or orange in the eyes around the pupil does not mean they are warm. Many Winters have this characteristic.	Soft cool brown
eye patterns:	**eye patterns:**
Black spikes and spokes (usually at top) from pupil to iris edge	Combination of Winter and Summer characteristics
Most common in brown or hazel eyes	
Heavy orange or yellow splash for some hazel eyes	
Other overlapping seasonal patterns	

SUMMER	SPRING	AUTUMN
skin tones—cool or blue undertone:	**skin tones—yellow or warm undertone:**	**skin tones—yellow or warm undertone:**
Porcelain (very fair)	Ivory or milky white (some with freckles)	Ivory to light beige (sometimes with freckles)
Pink	Peach (some with freckles)	Peach
Rose beige (tans easily)	Beige or golden beige	Ruddy (with peach, pink, or red)
Ruddy with pink or red	Ruddy with peach, pink, or red (high color in cheeks, chin, and sometimes forehead)	Golden beige or coppery bronze
Beige with hint of sallow (yellow)		
hair color:	**hair color:**	**hair color:**
Platinum blonde	Blonde—golden, honey, or flaxen	Strawberry blonde
Ash or smoky blonde	Strawberry blonde	Ash blonde with gold highlights
Ash brown (light to medium)	Red	Red to auburn
Sandy or soft brown with blonde highlights	Brown—light to medium with gold or red highlights	Golden brown to dark auburn brown
Silver gray	Gray to creamy gray	Creamy white
Creamy gray (appears to have natural blonde highlights)	*Note: Blonde hair may be highlighted, and red shades are best colored in red tones.*	Sometimes black
Note: The ash-toned hair frosts or highlights beautifully.		*Note: Most Autumn hair shades are best colored in the same solid hair color as the natural color.*
eye color:	**eye color:**	**eye color:**
Blue, gray-blue, or soft gray	Clear blue (gray blue sometimes), aqua, or teal blue	Dark brown
Gray green, yellow green, or aqua	Light brown, golden brown (topaz brown)	Red brown to golden brown
Hazel, soft cool brown, or grayed brown	Hazel	Green with gold, pale green, olive green
No dark brown	No dark brown eyes	Hazel
		Teal blue, aqua blue
eye patterns:	**eye patterns:**	**eye patterns:**
Lacy or cracked glass pattern	Sunlight effect from small space or donut shape around pupil	Flower petal or star shape around pupil
Webbing effect or tear-drop shape	Some cracked glass shapes	Similarities to Summer cracked glass pattern
Soft opaque with white-effect radiating from pupil in some blue eyes	Some closely resemble other seasonal patterns	
Some overlapping seasonal patterns		

FRECKLES

Any season, warm or cool, may be freckled. Just remember, the cool skins with freckles will appear more blended than the warm skins with freckles; the warm skins are usually more heavily freckled.

I've seen both Springs and Autumns draped as Summers because the consultant's goal was to blend the freckles away. She accomplished her goal, but it was at the expense of taking away the radiance in the warm skin. Good healthy color should never be sacrificed just to gain softness. We all need the best of both worlds.

THE DIFFERENCE COLOR MAKES

Once your season has been determined and you start wearing your colors, you will begin to receive compliments on your appearance. This new, attractive you will result in a new self-confidence as you begin to develop your own sense of personal style.

The colors that you wear should promote, compliment, and harmonize the undertone coloring in your hair, skin, and eyes. In other words, a cool or blue-undertoned skin must wear a cool or blue-undertoned color, and a warm or yellow-undertoned skin must wear a warm or yellow-undertoned color.

In considering which seasonal palette is best for the cool undertone, you must first look at the amount of contrast between hair and skin tone. The higher the contrast between hair and skin, the more dramatic the Winter person becomes. A Winter person wears black and white better than anyone else because it plays up the contrast between hair and skin. As the hair color lightens to medium brown with fair to light skin tones, this person may be more flattered by the cool saturated tones of Winter II. In some color systems, this person would be referred to as a soft or lower-contrast Winter or a high-contrast or bright Summer which is why she is often draped as a Winter and other times as a Summer.

The darker cool skin tones in the olive or black skin category with dark brown to black hair will look best in the cool bright and darker hues of the Winter I palette. The Winter I person does not have high skin-to-hair contrast, just darker coloring overall.

The Spring and Autumn palettes beautifully accommodate warm skin tones. A Spring person wears more delicate colors in a lower contrast of warm tints with light to medium values. An Autumn person needs the richer, more saturated, and somewhat contrasted tones and shades of the warm undertones.

The Spring person with lower contrast of skin to hair is beautifully balanced in the Spring colors whereas Autumn may have very fair to richer coloring in coppery to black skin tones. Autumn has more variety in skin and hair color than Spring. Autumn is the best choice when you can't decide whether Spring or Autumn is better. Autumns can wear some Spring colors, but Springs can never wear Autumn colors successfully.

Depending upon the depth of coloring, a clear Winter palette or soft Summer palette will be most complimentary to the cool undertone, and a clear Spring palette or an earthy Autumn palette will be most complimentary to the warm undertone.

Surface skin color often disguises the undertone. This is due to melanin, which enables the skin to tan easily. The less melanin, the quicker the skin burns in the sun and the more transparent the skin is. Therefore, olive and darker skins with high-melanin content disguise their undertone almost completely; however, these individuals are usually blue-based. Many of these skins become sallow; they have a sickly yellow cast with gray shadows as they respond to yellow or golden-based colors. Thus, blue-based colors will bring a healthier quality to this skin, as well as to their hair and eyes. Many beige skins are sallow as well.

The warm skins will sometimes deceive because they can have a pinky quality in the face, especially if ruddy (high-color). Generally warm skins are peachy, ivory, or coppery in quality.

DETERMINING YOUR SEASON

The draping of colored fabrics around the neck and shoulder area is the best technique to determine a person's coloring. When I color drape an individual, it is always without make-up. I'm looking for that person to be totally promoted by the color. This means that not only is

the skin tone complimented by color, but the natural hair color is richer and the eyes are brighter and more alive.

A second way to determine undertone is to lay one hand against orange matte fabric and the other against a fuchsia matte fabric, or against gold and silver lamé fabric. The cool skin tone looks healthier with less redness in the knuckles on the cool color. The veins are less obvious and the skin less yellow on the fuchsia or silver. Whereas the warm hand will usually have white areas between the knuckles which often look pink or blue gray in color on the fuchsia or silver. On the warm colors, the cool undertone appears very yellow and redness stands out. The yellow undertone picks up color in the whiter areas and knuckles and veins blend better on warm colors.

The Winter skin will appear brightened and healthy in Winter colors. The Summer skin will appear soft and somewhat transparent in Summer colors. The Spring skin will be and must look radiant in Spring colors. The Autumn skin will appear warm and coppery in the Autumn colors.

NEGATIVE EFFECTS OF COLOR

The wrong colors will dull the skin, hair, and eyes. The person usually becomes one with the color, or pulls down into the color, thus aging the face immediately! If the person appears tired, dull, and unhealthy, or the skin texture appears coarse, or if the coloring in the face pales and separates into blotchy patches, then the color around the face is definitely wrong. If the attention is drawn to the nose, mouth, chin, or jaw, then the color is also wrong.

The best adjective used to describe negative response to color is "drag." The wrong colors for anyone causes the face to drag down into the color. This dragging effect on the face causes the person to look older, tired, and unhealthy.

Good color always lifts the face, drawing attention toward sparkling eyes. The skin looks as though foundation has been reapplied, thus creating a smooth texture and an evenness of color. Not even a facelift can restore the color of youth, but the use of seasonal palettes can greatly enhance a plastic surgeon's work.

THE HAIR COLOR FACTOR

The most common mistake made today is changing the natural hair color to a much lighter than natural shade or completely into another undertone. Picture Joan Collins with Barbara Mandrell's or Bonnie Franklin's hair color, or Donna Mills with Ali McGraw's or Cher's hair color. You cannot soften high contrast without destroying the drama and appeal, and likewise to darken a soft or gentle look without creating a hardened or stark appearance.

One last comment to those of you who are graying or maturing. Don't be misled to believe that you must now lighten your hair. Look carefully at how your natural hair color is changing and stay within the parameters of your natural coloring. Don't overcompensate. Either maintain your natural high contrast of hair to skin tone for brightness or your low-contrast coloring to maintain your gentle radiance.

The correct colors *lift* the face and brighten the hair and eyes. The wrong colors will create a drag on the face, pulling it down into the color worn. When drag occurs, the face either blends into the color or shadows, flaws, or blotchy areas darken and expression lines deepen; thus the person appears aged or unhealthy.

Remember, God gave you a "package deal" in creating hair, skin, and eyes that are all in natural *balance* within the same color base. Maintaining this *natural* balance is the only way to maximize your natural beauty.

CHOOSING A GOOD COLOR ANALYST

Much has been written, publicized, and said about the benefits of color analysis.

As we consider the benefits of color, we find much has been written on the subject of color analysis. Today, many women have even had their "colors done" several times because they were dissatisfied with the original results. Sometimes it is at the urging of a friend, or perhaps just because it's fun—especially if it doesn't cost anything and a "make-up party" is involved.

Does any of this sound familiar? The sad thing is that the end result, because of differing opinions each time, is frustration and/or a discrediting to the whole field of color analysis in the mind of the "victim."

So how do you decide who is right or where to go for an accurate color analysis? The following are some criteria you should consider when determining the credibility of an analyst.

■ A good color analyst recognizes that the *skin response to color is the key* to determining seasonal colors. The response of the natural hair color and eyes to having particular colors draped under an individual's face and across the shoulders must also be considered.

■ A good color analyst seeks to place her client in colors that "lift and promote" that client's face and natural hair color balance. For example, an individual may have cool *soft* ash hair and a pink transparent quality to her complexion. Bold cool colors will only overpower this person, whereas a soft, dusty cool color will give her good balance to the color worn and a healthy, youthful complexion.

■ A good analyst is careful to use natural or simulated "natural" lighting. Care should be taken to make sure the light is evenly diffused on the face, eliminating any unnatural shadows. Be aware that fluorescent or incandescent lights that are in the draping area can throw an unnatural color on the skin tone. Natural or good simulated natural light gives the best results.

■ A good analyst uses color drapes that have proven to be good test colors. These drapes should represent each of those hues that consistently show well on everyone. An excellent test between a Winter person and a Summer person is charcoal gray versus charcoal blue gray or true red versus summer red.

■ A good analyst first determines whether her client has a cool blue-based undertone or a warm yellow-based undertone. Rose-pink versus orange is the best test. If the undertone is difficult to determine, then make-up application is extremely helpful at this point.

Warm make-up should be placed on one side of the face: foundation, blush, lip color, and eye color. The same amount of cool make-up should be placed in the same places on the other side. The analyst will look at the client directly face forward. There will be a lift to the correct side, a drag to the other.

The correct make-up for the client's skin tone will look at home on her face; it will blend beautifully. The wrong make-up will seem to set on the surface of the skin without blending well. This is a great test if natural light is unavailable or still has not revealed the better response. Once this is done, it can be determined which seasonal palette of color is best in the client's undertone.

I find this procedure to be more accurate, and it results in fewer mistakes. A good analyst will also help her client see her skin's responses to the test colors as draping occurs.

■ A good analyst recommends the colors that give the most healthy, flawless appearance to the skin, make the eyes sparkle, and add richness to the natural hair color.

■ The good analyst should ask if the hair color has been changed or oxidized by a permanent or the sun. Then the hair must be covered to prevent a false indication with the drape colors. All too often redness or golden qualities in the hair are the results of external influences, rather than inborn traits. Too many clients and consultants make incorrect observations by choosing warm colors that enhance this "unnatural" feature.

I was incorrectly analyzed the first time because, when I was 24 years old, I made myself a golden blonde. When I was draped, I told the consultant my natural brown hair had reddish highlights. As a result, I was draped as a Spring. However, I am a Winter II.

■ A good analyst teaches her client proper skin care and make-up techniques and recommends the best color choices for her cosmetics.

- A good analyst redrapes her client after cosmetics are applied, verifying the rightness of the colors chosen and allowing her client to see how wonderful this complete harmony with color, cosmetics, and her natural attributes can be.

  At this point in the consultation, the analyst should give personal recommendations as to the best colors and the least flattering colors in her seasonal palette. This information should be supplied to you if you are paying for a complete color/make-up consultation. Remember, you will receive the best results from someone who is a trained color consultant, not a "make-up" consultant. The consultant's emphasis should be servicing her client's needs.

- A good color analyst should have received a minimum of 16 hours of in-depth seasonal color training where she had the opportunity to do hands-on draping and also observed a large number of people draped. Instructional information is not nearly enough by itself. Also, videos are not a substitute for live models! Too many TVs do not have good color balance.

- A good color analyst should have gone through a color certification test. Obviously, these criteria are also important when choosing someone to train you in color analysis. Don't pay for a color consultation without finding out what and how the service will be rendered, along with the consultant's background and training. Even the best are in danger of becoming lax at times. This is a field where consultants must keep their techniques fine-tuned. I believe "if you don't use it, you can lose it." Realizing this fact, a good training firm will offer refresher courses to their consultants. Experience is a great teacher, but newer consultants can easily get onto a "wrong track" in their draping.

NOTES

CHAPTER TWO

HOW DO I DRESS
THIS BODY?

Like so many adolescents, I did not like the body God gave me. My waist was too big; my hips were too flat; and my legs were not shapely enough. It seemed as though all my friends had perfect "little" figures. Actually, as I think back, I would have been happier if I had been born in the 1800s when women wore corsets and long, full dresses. That would have disguised all my "flaws"! Well, as I have learned over and over again, God's plan and timing in our lives is always perfect. Now, I wouldn't change my time and place for anything.

My flaws have kept me humble and much more able to relate to other women, who are just as critical of themselves as I am of myself. It took many years of my adult life to come to understand that my frame can never be changed, no matter how thin I get or how much exercise I do.

As I worked with color analysis and make-up, I realized that was only the beginning of image development. I would hear retailers complain about "these women with their color charts" coming in to their stores and having no idea about style and line, just wanting anything in the right "color." That prompted me to put together a total image program. I observed women's shapes and found that there were similarities in their overall frames and that there were some basic frames that most bodies resembled.

In college, we measured to determine size and shape, and I came to realize that most women are intimidated by measuring tapes. The thought that other women might know their bust, waist, and hip sizes, especially if their measurements increase as they descend the body, is horrifying! As a home economics major, with an emphasis in clothing, textiles, and design, I began to see how clothing styles and lines can enhance or destroy any figure. For many years, I sewed and tailored all my clothes, particularly suits and dresses; I learned what lines flattered my figure.

So my conclusion was that we need to correct what appears to be disproportionate. Most figure challenges can be disguised—even excessive weight problems can be minimized visually. Knowing this now makes me want to take each woman I see with a low self-image and say "I can help you!"

Everybody has potential for attractiveness. In fact, there are very few natural beauties, if that is of any comfort. As Jean Lush, author of *Emotional Phases of a Woman's Life,* has said, "Today's woman has no excuse not to be attractive." Never has there been a time in history when women have had so many tools available to create beauty. As recently as 30 years ago, you were either blessed with attractive attributes or you were not. Today's woman, however, can only claim laziness or lack of interest if she has not developed her potential. That's why I'm so glad God placed me in this time and place. I have every possible advantage for hair care, skin care, cosmetics, clothing styles, and fabric choices.

Even extra weight is not an excuse for a lack of style and attractiveness. Many women who are overweight feel they do not deserve to spend money on themselves; they punish themselves by looking dumpy. They don't realize they are also punishing those they care about by setting a poor example and lowering their self-image. A vicious cycle develops. Year after year, they talk about losing weight and, because their motivation gradually fails, they never do. Thus the best years of their lives pass them by while they wait for the right time and the right diet. Sometimes a cynical attitude is the end result, and this only destroys relationships. I pray this is not your plight. If it is, however, take heart. Begin to develop your look at your current weight. Stop waiting for tomorrow or next year and learn how to dress the body you have and enjoy life today!

Whatever your figure challenges, there are good clothing lines for them all. Don't look to the retail store clerks for good advice. Most sales people will not be honest with you because their first priority is sales for the store. Besides, they do not know you, your personality, lifestyle, etc. In all fairness, there are those exceptional clerks who have a good eye for proportion or who have had some image training. However, these people are definitely in the minority.

Once I learned that I could disguise all the "flaws" that concerned me, I became much less self-conscious and much more people conscious. I forgot about how I look from other angles and directed my thoughts to the task at hand. It is a liberating feeling to learn how to successfully dress your figure.

If you have already found an attractive hairstyle, achieved your best look with cosmetics, and learned what colors really compliment you, then the next step in developing your personal style is learning how to balance your figure with good lines and proportion.

CLOTHING LINES AND FABRICS THAT FLATTER YOUR FIGURE

I am amazed at how often women choose clothes that add pounds to their appearance. Principles of good proportion and balance are really very simple. Anyone can learn them. So, if you want to look thinner or even heavier, this chapter offers you the answers you are seeking.

There is a tremendous amount of illusion involved in the development of good proportion. The primary goal of any clothing is to create a balanced body. Therefore, the first question you should ask yourself when you try on any garment is *"Does this balance my figure frame?"*

THE IMPORTANCE OF LINE AND PROPORTION

Every garment has three major sets of lines that affect the figure. **Body lines** make up the first set. These lines are created by the seams, darts, tucks, etc. They provide the fit and contour of the garment.

Silhouette lines make up the second set of lines. These are formed by the basic shape of the garment. A sheath silhouette creates the illusion of slimness and height unless the garment is closely fitted where there is a figure challenge. An A-line silhouette will hide a full or wide hip and derrière, slimming the figure. It also balances a full bust or wide shoulders. A chemise of unshaped silhouette will cause the figure to look taller and slimmer as well as hide a thick waist if need be. A blouson or dropped-waist silhouette can balance or conceal problems like a short, thick waist and full bust.

Detail lines make up the third set of lines. They are formed by the pattern detail on the garment, such as repeated horizontal, vertical, or curved lines. **Horizontal lines** will create an illusion of width, and thus a shorter figure. Visualize a shorter figure with lots of horizontal lines. This figure will look shorter and heavier than it actually is, especially if these lines are placed at fuller parts of the body. A singular horizontal line can create the illusion of more height if placed above or below the median line of the body (see Figure A). Shoulder yokes will add width across the shoulder or bustline. All hemlines—whether on the skirt, overblouse, jacket, or vest—should be at a flattering level, not at a figure challenge.

A **vertical line** usually makes the person look taller and slimmer, particularly if it is a singular line because this leads the eye upward. However, if the vertical line is repeated several times, it can lead the eye horizontally, especially if the lines are not close together. A garment with a single vertical line down the center front with buttons is very slimming, as well as a solid, unbroken color (See Figure B). Other slimming vertical lines include princess seaming, pleats, and gored shapes, depending upon their placement.

Diagonal and curved lines can be very slimming if the angles are deep enough. A shorter angle will give the impression of width (See Figure C). Any line that disguises figure

SILHOUETTE LINES

A-line, sheath, chemise, blouson.

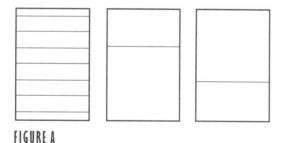

FIGURE A

Horizontal lines.

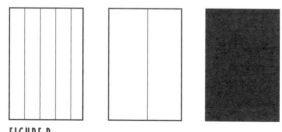

FIGURE B

Vertical lines.

challenges is a flattering line. Any line that draws attention to your figure challenges is a negative line.

Finally, we often forget that a negative line placed at a fuller part of the figure need not be avoided, if we place a flattering line at a smaller part of the figure for balance.

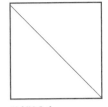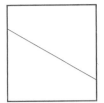

FIGURE C

Diagonal lines.

THE EFFECTS OF PATTERN, COLOR, AND FABRIC TEXTURE

The **size of the pattern** on a garment will also affect the appearance of the weight and size of the body. For example, if a figure is surrounded by large items it appears smaller or even dwarfed. But if a figure is surrounded by small items, it appears larger (See Figure D).

So, if a large woman puts on a small print, she will look larger. If a small woman wears a large print, she will look smaller and even overwhelmed. By the same token, a small face in large earrings will look even smaller and vice versa. Remember to carry out this principle as you apply jewelry to the body. A large woman needs larger necklaces or pins, nothing small or dainty.

Color and its optical illusions must be considered at the same time. If a large print is placed on a large woman for correct balance, it should not be in such bright colors as red, orange, or yellow

BALANCING LINES

Shoulder pads balance peplums.

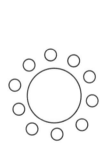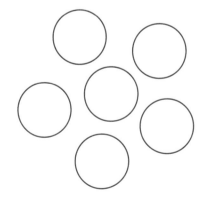

FIGURE D

Illusions created by pattern—The circles in the middle of each grouping are the same size, but the circle in the middle of the small circles appears larger.

because these colors increase apparent size and attract the eye first. Contrasting color patterns will do the same thing.

If the colors used are in the blue, green, or violet family, they can actually reduce the size of the figure. Muted colors also tend to recede and reduce the apparent figure size.

In our discussion of proportion, we also need to consider **fabric.** Bulky fabrics, such as coarse tweeds, widewale corduroys, heavy wools, and nubby knits, will give the impression of added weight. Crisp or stiff fabrics, like taffeta, heavy poplin, or duck cloth, will stand away from the body and hide some imperfections, but again they add the appearance of extra weight if there is much volume to the fabric.

Shiny fabrics like satin or charmeuse reflect light and cause the body to look heavier. On the other hand, matte textures absorb light and are the best choices for the larger figure. Matte fabrics include flat knits, gabardines, crepe, challis, etc. These fabrics are good for every figure, small or large.

Ideally fabric should hang well on the figure without clinging to any bulges. The more rounded the figure, the drapier the fabric can be; the straighter the figure, the crisper the fabric can be.

Like body weight and shape, **hair** should also be considered when selecting fabric textures. The wrong fabric weight and/or the wrong shade can destroy a woman's hair texture and color instantly.

PLEASING PROPORTIONS

Long jacket/short skirt, short jacket/long pants, short jacket/ long skirt.

As you know by now, proportion is most pleasing when good overall *balance* is achieved. It is most pleasing when areas on the figure are unevenly divided to create interest. Examples of this would be found in combinations of jackets or tops with pants or skirts. That is why we see longer jackets with shorter skirts and shorter jackets with fuller pants or long skirts.

As you look at the proportion of any garment, you need to ask if it will flatter your positive features and conceal the negative ones. You also should evaluate the use of color, print, fabric, and design.

TYPES OF BODY FRAMES/BONE STRUCTURE

A-FRAME

- Body appears narrower at top half and wider at the lower hip and upper thigh area.

- Spine may be swaybacked with a protruding derrière.

- Legs may be shorter and sometimes heavier.

- Upper torso may be average to long—firm and slender.

- Bust is usually average to small, rarely large.

- Figure can remain very youthful if there is no tendency to gain weight.

- First few pounds are gained in the upper thigh area.

This frame should be balanced by widening the shoulders. This can be achieved by choosing garments that have shoulder pads or sleeve detailing.

V-FRAME

- Shoulders appear to be obviously wider than hips.

- Bust is usually large with shorter waist and high hips.

- Appearance is top heavy.

- Thighs and derrière are usually flat.

- Legs are normally thin.

- Tummy may be more prominent than bust; in fact, upper torso may be barrel-shaped.

- First few pounds are gained in the upper torso area.

This frame should be balanced by widening the hip and upper leg area. This would entail choosing garments that have width and fullness in the skirt or pants.

THE A-FRAME.

THE V-FRAME.

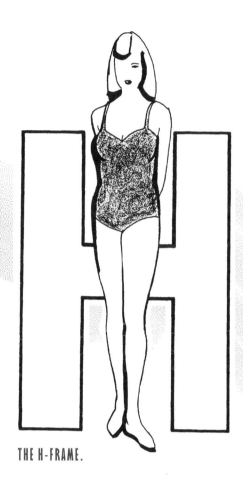

THE H-FRAME.

H-FRAME

- Body appears to be fairly straight up and down.

- Thighs and derrière are usually flat.

- Waist is usually thicker, giving a straighter appearance to figure.

- Legs may be longer.

- Bust may be average to large.

- Weight gain is usually through the middle—waist and tummy before thighs and lower hips.

This frame should be balanced by creating the illusion of a smaller waist or disguising it altogether. This can be accomplished by choosing either a bloused garment with a flared skirt and belted waist or a straight garment like a chemise dress.

8-FRAME

- Frame is curvy and perfectly balanced.

- Bust is full, and waist is small with average length.

- Hips are gently tapered with good proportions to derrière.

- Leg length and upper torso length are balanced.

- Weight gain is always evenly distributed.

This figure should emphasize the waist and avoid cluttering the figure with lots of clothes or layers. This would involve choosing garments that fit the body and identify the waist.

CREATING BALANCE

If you are attempting to analyze your own figure, stand in front of a full-length mirror and simply look for the obvious shapes and lengths. Start with your neck—remember that the neck appears longer on sloping shoulders and shorter on square ones.

If you found that you have some characteristics from more than one category, then you simply have a combination frame or a frame that is balanced. Just follow the recommendations for your figure challenges and remember to create good balance from top to bottom.

THE 8-FRAME.

Now that we have looked at some of the principles of line and proportion, we need to consider the figure and any possible problems. Major figure challenges are obvious to others, but, with the right techniques, they can be minimized or disguised. Here are a few:

- long neck
- short neck and double chin
- round or sloping shoulder (emphasizes extra weight)
- broad shoulders
- thin arms (bony)
- heavy arms or flabby arms
- small bust/flat chest
- full/low bust
- thick waist
- short waist

- long waist
- protruding tummy (more prominent than bustline)
- wide hips (just below the waist)
- large upper thighs or saddlebags
- protruding derrière
- flat derrière
- short legs
- thin legs
- large calves/thick ankles

Minor figure challenges are noticed only by you and are often imagined to be major problems. The only time someone else notices them is when you tell, and even then that person will probably say she'd never noticed it before! If you learn to do a good job of disguising a major figure challenge, no one else will ever see it unless you verbally call attention to it.

NECKS

If you visually have a long neck, you should avoid short hair that exposes the back of your neck. As you consider what necklines to wear, remember they frame your face and create a direction for the eye to follow. High necklines shorten the neck because they carry the eye upward.

FLATTERING CHOICES FOR LONG NECKS

Turtlenecks, accessories, cowl necks.

■ long necks

flattering choices:	unflattering choices:
high collars (mandarin, stand-up, and Cossack collars)	short hair and low necklines
turtlenecks	
cowl necks	
accessories include chokers, necklaces, ribbons, or scarves	

■ short necks

flattering choices:	unflattering choices:
open collars	clutter around the neck
shawl collars	any high-neck styles
V-necklines	
short hairstyles	

(These lines bring the eye downward and lengthen the neck.)

FLATTERING CHOICES FOR SHORT NECKS

V-neck, shawl collar, square neckline.

HEADSET

Another feature to consider is your "headset." Is it forward from the side view of your body or is it even with it? If your headset is forward, then choose to wear your hair full in the back of the neck, as well as collars to disguise it nicely.

SHOULDERS

As you observe your neck, you may notice that your shoulders are sloping, square, or tapered. Obviously, if you have sloping or **narrow shoulders,** you need shoulder pads. The type of pads you choose depends on the garment's sleeve style. If the sleeve is a set-in style, then you need a cutoff shoulder pad. This is currently the most popular style as the trend in fashion moves toward a softer, more natural look. However, regardless of what may be happening in fashion, shoulder pads will always be a must for most mature women because they can take as much as 15 pounds and 15 years off your figure.

If you have **broad shoulders,** you should still wear shoulder pads—thin shoulder pads. They detract from the shoulder and arm that is "fleshy" and full, and they cause the garment to hang nicely. Don't worry about having "football shoulders"—instead look at the positive results!

The average shoulder can wear almost any style sleeve, however, the raglan sleeve does cause the shoulder's appearance to drop forward. Shoulder pads can help correct this look.

■ narrow shoulders ■

flattering choices:	unflattering choices:
shallow/wide necklines, such as boat necks	raglan sleeves
horizontal patterns on the shoulders	dolman, batwing, kimono, and peasant sleeves
set-in sleeves	deep or narrow necklines
puffed sleeves	
detail on the shoulder edges	
cap sleeves	
fabrics that do not droop or cling to the shoulders	
wider lapels that point upward	

FLATTERING CHOICES FOR NARROW SHOULDERS

(clockwise from bottom left to center) Horizontal shoulder, cap sleeves, shawl collar, shoulder details, upward-pointing lapels, puffed sleeves.

UNFLATTERING CHOICES FOR NARROW SHOULDERS

Deep V-necks, peasant sleeves, no sleeves, kimono sleeves.

**FLATTERING
CHOICES FOR
BROAD SHOULDERS**

Downward-pointing collar,

peasant sleeves, vertical

lines, deep V-neck.

▪broad shoulders ━━━━━━━━━━

flattering choices:	unflattering choices:
dolman, batwing, kimono, and peasant sleeves	boat necks
vertical stripes or tucks	puffed sleeves
deep/narrow necklines	detail on shoulder edges
narrower lapels that point downward	
collars scaled to shoulder size for balance	

BUSTLINES

The bustline should be firm and rounded in appearance. That should tell you immediately that a good-fitting bra is crucial! (Next to a good hairstyle, a good bra is the most important feature involved in a good self-image.)

When I help a woman shop for the first time, we always begin in the foundations department because a good-fitting bra can change the way her clothes fit.

Principle number one in fitting a bra is to find one that supports you without tightening the straps. Generally, this means an underwire style is needed. The straps are not to function like a harness that holds you in place; instead, their purpose is to smooth the cups. So, if you have red indentation marks under your bra straps, this indicates your bra is not supporting your breasts, but your straps are. Also, there should be no flesh bulging in front of the cups.

The second principle in fitting your bra is that it should hold your bustline no more than 3" below your armpit. Sports or natural bras do not flatter most women; they cause the breasts to swing out to the sides, flatten, and drop. Obviously, their purpose is not for support.

If you are **large-busted,** that is you wear a size D or larger, there are certain garment lines that will flatter your figure more than others. To avoid having to buy clothing that is one to two sizes larger than the rest of your body, choose a style that has a shoulder yoke with gathers or small pleats in the bodice of the garment.

Large-breasted women should try to avoid looking matronly or top heavy. One flattering bodice line is the surplice wrap or "cross your heart" style. If you wear a DD or larger, then you should shop for a bra minimizer. This will give you good support and reduce the apparent size of your bust. It will definitely take pounds off and give your figure a more youthful appearance.

The **small-busted** woman has more of an advantage in selecting clothing than the large-busted one. She does not have the limitations as to what she can wear; her goal is to fill out the bustline. One of her options would be the contemporary "push-up" style bra which will create a more shapely, fuller bustline.

FLATTERING CHOICES FOR LARGE BUSTS

V-neck, shawl collar, diagonal lines, no lapels.

■ large busts

flattering choices:	unflattering choices:
V-necks	horizontal lines at the bust
small lapels or none at all	high-waisted looks
shawl collars	stiff fabrics
vertical or diagonal lines	tube tops or anything tight
single small button fronts on softly tailored blouses	patch breast pockets
	smocking at the bust
	large ruffles or bows at the bustline
	wide belts

UNFLATTERING CHOICES FOR LARGE BUSTS

(clockwise from left)
Horizontal lines at bust, details at bust, tight top with large belt, ruffles at bust, patch breast pockets.

flattering choices:	unflattering choices:
blousy designs	garments that are flat in bodice
layers of clothing	
pockets at the bust	
details in the bust area that express personal style	
padded bras (push-up styles will benefit your figure the most)	

UNFLATTERING CHOICES FOR SMALL BUSTS

Flat bodice with cap sleeves, dropped lapels.

FLATTERING CHOICES FOR SMALL BUSTS

(clockwise from bottom left) Blousy design, bulky fabric, layers, patch breast pockets.

WAISTS

The day of the small waist is long gone. Today's average waistline is 27" to 28", with 25" considered to be small. If you have a tapered hip, then more than likely you have an average to long waistline that is small in comparison to the rest of your figure, and your rib cage is probably slender as well. You are the lucky one who can have lots of fun with belts of various widths. If you are **thick-waisted,** don't assume you cannot wear belts. Everyone can wear them; they just wear them differently. The thick waist is usually accompanied by a wider rib cage and a short-to-average waist length.

If you have a thick waist, your goal is to either disguise it altogether by hiding it under a straight garment or to create a small waist appearance by blousing above and below a belted look. Either can be done if you are not too overweight. Just remember, measurement is not important. Appearance is what you need to be concerned about.

If your pantyhose are too tight, too long, or too short, they can distort your waistline. If they are too tight or if you need to roll the waist over to take up slack, you can simply clip the waist reinforcement to give more comfort. This technique works well with regular and light support hose. Ideally, you need to search for pantyhose that best fit your proportions.

Short-waisted figures find that one-piece garments are too long in the waist. They also find that a belt with any width at all tends to take up all the space between their bust and waist. If this is your problem, then try wearing separates instead of one-piece garments. When wearing a blouse with a skirt or pants, make sure you blouse the top over the waist to lengthen its appearance.

To visually determine if you are short-waisted, drop your arm to your side with the palm of your hand facing forward. If the crease on the front side of your elbow lines up within 1" of your waist, you are average-waisted. However, if your elbow crease falls more than 1" below the waist, you are short-waisted.

Long-waisted figures find that most one-piece garments are not long enough in the waist. To visually determine if you are long-waisted, use the same procedure as for the short waist. The elbow crease will fall more than 1" above the natural waistline.

FLATTERING CHOICES FOR THICK WAISTS

Overblouse, long jacket, front focal point at waist center, chemise, dropped blouson-style dress, vest, ornate belt.

■thick waists

flattering choices:	unflattering choices:
1½" belts (same color as the garment)	drawing attention to the entire waist
belt buckle as a focal point	contrast at the waistline
slacks with pleats and pressed creases	
high- or low-waisted styles	
tunic tops	
overblouse	
Chanel-style jackets	
chemises	
loose vests or cardigan sweaters	
dropped blouson-style dresses	
one-piece bathing suits	
no contrast between top and bottom	

flattering choices:	unflattering choices:
narrow belts (no smaller than 1", no larger than 1½")	wide waistbands
stiff back self-belts with buckles	wide belts (more than 1½" wide)
belts that match the top garment, not the bottom	bare midriff
unfitted jackets	tight-fitting tops
overblouse	short jackets
longer open vests	horizontal lines on the bodice
tunics (if tall enough)	high-waisted pants or skirts
outfits of one color	contrasting colors at the waist
loose layers	

FLATTERING CHOICES FOR SHORT WAISTS

Loose layers, one color garment, dropped waist dress, tunic.

UNFLATTERING CHOICES FOR SHORT WAISTS

Short jacket, high-waisted garment, wide belt.

flattering choices:	unflattering choices:
belts that match the bottom garment, not the top	low-rise pants
wide belts	dropped-waist styles
blouses tucked in, pulled out only when belted	low-slung belts
Empire-styled waists	overblouse
tops with yokes	blousons
tops with horizontal stripes or pockets	short hemlines, if also short-legged
	narrow belts

FLATTERING CHOICES FOR LONG WAISTS

Belt matches bottom garment, high-waisted garment, yoke with horizontal stripe, wide belt.

UNFLATTERING CHOICES FOR LONG WAISTS

Blouson style with short-cropped pants, long top with short skirt, low-slung belt, long overblouse, dropped waist garment.

HIPS

There are two hip problems: one is the high, wide hip and the other is the low hip or "saddlebag problem." Our goal with either is to disguise it! The **wide, high hip** often has a thick waist. The **low hip** usually has a slender rib cage with a nice waistline tapering gradually onto the hips. There are many figures that have a modification of both problems, and this can give a more balanced figure as long as the other areas of the body are not out of proportion.

■wide hips

flattering choices:	unflattering choices:
modified dirndl skirts (about 3" of ease into waistband)	pockets at the hipline
vertical lines from the waist down	large plaids
shoulder pads to balance hips	horizontal lines at the waist and hips
pants with pressed creases	narrow shoulder lines
belts worn slightly above the waist	clingy/fitted tops
control-top pantyhose (takes 5 pounds off the figure)	wide belts
	full dirndl skirts
	straight box pleats
	widewale corduroy pants or skirts
	tight pants
	clingy fabrics
	back pockets
	front/rear patch pockets

FLATTERING CHOICES FOR WIDE HIPS

Shoulder pads, vertical lines below waist, blousy top, modified dirndl skirt, flared skirt with a dropped waist.

UNFLATTERING CHOICES FOR WIDE HIPS

Pockets at hipline, narrow top, full dirndl skirt, horizontal stripes at hips, large plaid pants, back pockets, widewale corduroy pants, tight pants with a short cropped top.

flattering choices:	unflattering choices:
A-line or flared skirts	pockets on the hips
long vest or jackets	excessive fullness in skirts or pants
moderately tapered or fitted jackets	pants that cup under derrière
sleeves that are narrow at the wrist	pants or skirts that are too tight
shoulder pads to balance the hips	horizontal lines at hips
gentle swing coats (three-quarters or longer)	pleated skirts
	bulky fabrics
	full gathered skirts

FLATTERING CHOICES FOR LOW HIPS

Trapeze top, A-line, long tapered jacket, shoulder pads, long jacket, swing coat.

UNFLATTERING CHOICES FOR LOW HIPS

Pants that cup under the derrière, pleats and pockets on hips, horizontal lines at hips, pleated skirt, too tight pants, too tight skirt.

STOMACHS

Most women believe they have a tummy problem; however, a real tummy problem exists only if it protrudes beyond the bustline. Correct posture would cure that problem for many of us. There are many garment styles that disguise or minimize the tummy.

FLATTERING CHOICES FOR ROUNDED TUMMIES

Focal point at face, overblouse, chemise, gored skirt, darts and soft pleats, waistless dress.

■ rounded tummies ■

flattering choices:	unflattering choices:
overblouse with a soft hang	full gathered skirts
pants with a soft pleat and dart combination	wide belts
chemise-style dresses	fly front on pants
flared or gored skirts	pleated skirts from the waist band
skirts with pleats that are sewn down	straight, bouffant, or gored skirts that cup under the tummy
flat strong fabrics	horizontal lines at the tummy
waistless dresses	clingy fabrics
focal point at the face	
pant zipper inside the left pocket	

**UNFLATTERING CHOICES
FOR ROUNDED TUMMIES**

Focal point at tummy,

skirt that cups under tummy,

horizontal lines at tummy,

fly front pants, wide belt,

clingy fabric.

DERRIÈRES

If your derrière extends beyond your shoulder blades from a figure profile perspective then you have a **protruding derrière.** The most common frustration in dressing this feature or challenge is the pants or skirt fitting too tightly with a waistband then that is too large. If you have this trait, you must avoid pants or skirts that *cup under* the derrière. Your goal is to choose garments that tastefully drape straight down from the fullest point of the derrière. Look also at inset pockets to make sure there is no gapping. To successfully dress this challenge you *must* step up a size and have the waistband altered to fit.

If your pants and straight skirts sag or bag in the "seat" area, then you have a **flat derrière.** Alterations in this area can often alleviate the sag, but ideally you should find those manufacturers who make pants and skirts to fit your shape. Your goal with this problem is to disguise it altogether or to create the illusion of more shape.

■ protruding derrières

flattering choices:	unflattering choices:
any skirt that flares from the waist	any line that defines and exposes this feature will enlarge it
any gathered skirt	
any A-line skirt	
any jacket with a full skirt	
a blazer-length jacket for fitted skirts or pants	
Note: Make sure your hemline is even front-to-back.	

flattering choices:	unflattering choices:
fullness to create shape off the waist on the backside	pants and skirts that sag or droop in the seat
tapered jackets	one-piece knits that cling
two-piece garments	pencil-slim skirts
blouses worn belted on the outside of pants or skirts	
peplums	
box jackets with full skirts	

**FLATTERING
CHOICES FOR FLAT
DERRIÈRES**

Fullness over
derrière, long jacket,
fullness on back,
box jacket with full
skirt, peplum.

**UNFLATTERING
CHOICES FOR FLAT
DERRIÈRES**

Saggy pants, clingy
one-piece knit garment,
pencil-slim skirt.

LEGS

Legs appear long or short depending on the length of the torso. A longer waist or torso will usually mean short legs are attached! If this is your case, your goal is to balance the lower body with the upper body.

FLATTERING CHOICES FOR SHORT LEGS

Longer skirt,

focal point at top,

high-waisted garment.

UNFLATTERING CHOICES FOR SHORT LEGS

Cuffs on pants.

■ short legs

flattering choices:	unflattering choices:
high heels (no more than 2½" unless you are tall)	cuffs on pants
high-waisted garments	
longer skirt hemlines	

▪ heavy legs

flattering choices:	unflattering choices:
straight- or full-leg pants	dainty pumps
pressed pant creases	strappy sandals
culotte skirts	thin, dainty shoes
2" to 3" heels	
matching skirt, hose, and shoes	
styles with a focal point at the neck or shoulders	
darker bottoms and lighter or brighter tops	

FLATTERING CHOICES FOR HEAVY LEGS

Light top with dark-bottoms and bottom-matching shoes and hose, split skirt, focal point at neck, straight-leg pressed pants.

FLATTERING CHOICES FOR LONG LEGS

Long-waisted style garment, long jacket, below-the-knee hem line, cuffs on pants, tunic, strappy sandals.

■ long legs

flattering choices:

long jackets that end below the crotch

tunics

long-waisted styles

cuffs on pants

straight skirt hems that fall just below the knee

dainty pumps

strappy sandals

thin high heels

unflattering choices:

dark hose

clunky shoes

skirts that are too long or
too short

high-waisted styles

ARMS

Whether you have thin or heavy arms, your goal is to disguise the size as much as possible.

FLATTERING CHOICES FOR HEAVY ARMS

Kimono sleeves, elbow-length sleeves, loose-fitting sleeves, long sleeves.

UNFLATTERING CHOICES FOR HEAVY ARMS

Clingy fabric, sleeveless blouse, puffed sleeves.

■ heavy arms

flattering choices:

loosely fitted sleeves

wide arm cuts

dolman or kimono sleeves are good if shoulder
pads are used

elbow-length or long sleeves

unflattering choices:

clingy fabrics

tight sleeves

sleeveless tops

puffy, cap, or short sleeves

cuffs on sleeves

■ thin arms

flattering choices:	unflattering choices:
sleeves that are wide and full above the elbow	tight sleeves
loose-fitting sleeves	tight turtleneck tops
bulky sleeves	cap sleeves
horizontal lines	sleeveless or strapless tops

FLATTERING CHOICES FOR THIN ARMS

Bulky sleeves, loose-fitting sleeves, sleeves that end well above the elbow.

UNFLATTERING CHOICES FOR THIN ARMS

Sleeveless dress, sleeveless turtleneck top, cap sleeves.

Once you learn to make the right choices for your garment lines, you will deceive the eyes of others all the time. No one will ever know what your figure challenges really are. This will bring greater satisfaction and confidence to your image development. Remember, you need to learn the rules first; then you can try breaking some of them with success. Just make sure that you rely on the trained eye that you are developing as you decide what works best for you.

GETTING INTO THE SWIM OF THINGS

To wear a swimsuit or not, that is the big question for so many women each and every spring or summer. We all have our reasons why we dread buying and wearing one. For some it is cellulite and protruding outer thighs, for others it is fat knees, a tummy, a thick waist, too much or too little bust. Some may have varicose veins, and although you can have injections that will cause them to disappear, I have always thought someone should design a bathing suit with leggings. Wouldn't that be perfect?! I believe I hear some of you laughing!

The lighting in most store dressing rooms is enough to discourage you before you have even finished trying on the first suit. It is very common for a woman to try on two dozen suits and never buy one. If this is your plight, all you need to know is what to look for in a suit style.

A-FRAME

The typical A-frame has a lower hip–outer thigh challenge. If you'd like your legs to appear longer and slimmer than they are, choose a French cut bathing suit, either one- or two-piece. If it is a two-piece, then choose the style that has the band at the waist. If you are long-waisted, this will give you the helpful horizontal line to shorten your waist and the Lycra fabric will help flatten the tummy. Ideally then the top should have a wide V-neckline into the shoulder strap or a horizontal line at the bust or shoulder to add the needed width for balance to the hips. If a one-piece is preferred, the same leg cut and neckline will be best. If you'd like to see a little more fullness in your bustline, wear a swimsuit that has ruffles or shaped cups at the bust.

FLATTERING SWIMSUIT CHOICES FOR THE A-FRAME

One-piece French cut, two-piece French cut with band at waist.

A FLATTERING SWIMSUIT CHOICE FOR LARGE BUSTS

A ruffle at the bottom.

A FLATTERING SWIMSUIT CHOICE FOR SMALL BUSTS

A ruffle at the top.

H-FRAME

If you'd like to deemphasize your waistline, select a one-piece suit with strong angled lines or curves. Built-in bras are great for the full- or small-busted woman. For women who deal with the embarrassment of nipple exposure, there are small 2½" to 3" pads that slip into the cups. They are available in some specialty shops or department stores.

A vertical line with shirred fabric down the left or right front of the suit will slim the figure. A V-front bodice design to below the waist will also slim the midriff area. If the fanny is flat, do not choose a European high-cut leg, especially if the legs are longer than the upper body. The fanny needs more coverage to be more flattered. Less angle to leg cut will accomplish this. If you are slim and short-waisted, then the bikini will lengthen your torso.

V-FRAME

The V-frame usually has two problems; a large, full bust and a flat fanny with a straighter waist line. A good bra top with a skirted style bottom would be best for needed balance. A surplice wrap-style top will give a very flattering line to the bust. Of course the curvy figure that is not heavy can do anything.

FLATTERING SWIMSUIT CHOICES FOR THICK WAISTS

V-front below the waist, a distracting contrast color at the bustline.

SHOPPING TIPS

■ When buying a bathing suit, choose one size larger than you normally wear in clothes. This gives you the needed length, not more width.

■ Name brands are building in tummy controls into their Lycra fabric suits.

■ European cuts expose the "buns," and American cuts do not.

■ Two-toned suits can be very flattering if the high-color contrast is from the bust line upward. This draws the eye to the face.

■ Beware of high contrast at the waist or hip line if you are thick-waisted or large-hipped.

■ Halter strap styles cannot be worn successfully on narrower sloping shoulders.

■ Become familiar with specialty shops or talk to buyers for bathing suit departments to learn about the various cuts of the different manufacturers.

COLOR TIPS

- Fair skins, regardless of season, should not wear black, white, navy, or extremely dark or light colors.

- Fair skins choose primary colors for the slimmer look.

- Dark skins look best in black, white, or extremely dark or light colors.

- Warm/peachy skins should choose periwinkles, corals, apple greens, mustards, or metallic golds for skin compliment.

NOTES

CHAPTER THREE

HOW DO I DISCOVER MY PERSONAL STYLE?

Your clothing personality is a very important part of your personal style. It is determined by your body structure and the type of hair and facial features you have. Your personality traits also influence your personal styles as that part of you is expressed in your look. Some people instinctively know what style or personality of clothes they feel "at home" in and truly express who they are. Others, because of being impressionable or due to their desire to please others, may even have a style dictated to them. This often happens to the professional, especially if she has a very conservative employer. It happens to people in the entertainment business and political arena every day. Clothing personality is a very important part of good personal style; however, it is not the only part.

THE BASIC PERSONALITY TYPES

There are six categories that are quite commonly used in reference to clothing styles—Classic, Dramatic, Romantic, Ingenue, Natural, and Gamin. You may find that one suits you perfectly or that you are a combination of two. Sometimes an influence of a third category enters the picture by way of fabric, pattern, or accessories. As you consider which one(s) describe your physical features and your personality traits, look carefully at your features before you choose it for yourself. If your body features are curvy like the Romantic, you cannot dress it with the boxy, tailored garments of the traditional Classic/Natural because you will appear matronly and heavier. On the other hand, if you have the straighter figure of the H-frame, soft flowing lines or fabrics that drape on the figure will cause your figure to appear dumpy or dowdy. You must choose a clothing style/personality that will flatter your figure as well as express your inner self.

THE CLASSIC

The Classic should be the epitome of elegance and refinement. The look is timeless but fashionable. Many Winters and Summers as well as some Springs and Autumns will be Classics. The Classic personality is controlled, not spontaneous, thus she rarely gets caught up in any passion of the moment. She loves and needs to be organized. Orderliness and structure in her work environment are important to her sense of well-being and freedom. In fact, chaos will almost always bring out the worst in her. Her calm, cool sophistication brings elegance and uplift to any business or social gathering. She's usually passionate about her work and is typically driven to be her best. She's usually very good in management or administrative positions because diplomacy is one of her attributes. Her friends are typically her social contacts through her work. From the time she's a young teen, she will express her heart and soul in her appearance. As a person she is warm and caring, always sincere. She will take her role of responsibility seriously.

THE CLASSIC
Eveningwear.

body type:

- Height will be in average range (5'4" to 5'7").

- Figure proportions will be evenly balanced and symmetrical.

- Overall appearance is mature adult, not "girlish."

- Body is not too thin, too delicate, or too sturdy.

facial features:

- Facial features are average to attractive.

- Features are symmetrical and evenly balanced. They are not long, wide, angular, or round.

hairstyle:

- Length will be moderate to somewhat short.

- Style should be well-groomed and controlled, *not* tousled and windblown.

- Cut will be either blunt and smooth or with some layering.

THE CLASSIC

Casualwear.

clothing style:

■ Styles will be fashionable and dignified, contemporary and upscale.

■ Lines are softly tailored or softly flowing.

■ Ensemble dressing is key to the look; mix-and-match does not create a Classic image.

■ Classics wear "dressmaker" style suits, not traditional "man-tailored" styles.

■ Classics styles are never trendy, faddish, or severe in style.

■ Solid colors dominate over prints in garment selection.

fabrics:

■ Matte finishes or low lusters are best for all key garments.

■ Richness and quality are key to her look.

■ Fabric weights are moderate.

■ Refined textures create the appropriate richness in silks, woolens (crepe, gabardine, or challis), cottons, and cashmere.

■ Smooth knits and double knits are also great.

accessories:

■ Jewelry, belts, handbags, and shoes should be refined, elegant, and fashionable.

■ Jewelry styles may be smooth circles or geometric in sleek or chunky styles.

■ Classics do not wear "dainty dangles" or funky styles.

Note: The Classic must be careful not to wear jewelry that is too dressy with her casual wear.

details:

■ Lines will be refined and smooth, slightly flared, or softly straight.

■ Necklines should be softly clean and simple or draped.

■ Any intricacy should be subdued—touches of lace are fine and a jacquard weave used in a blouse is a nice touch in some instances.

unflattering choices:

■ Boring and predictable dressing, too conservative styles.

■ Excessive angles as in severely tailored garments.

■ Very straight lines or oversized garments.

■ Dowdy or dumpy appearance caused by fabrics that are too drapey or too tailored.

■ Extreme shapes.

■ Heavy rough textures, stiff metallics, sheer fabrics, or clingy fabrics.

■ High color contrast or multicolor splashes in prints or patterns.

■ *Repeating* the *same look* or style season after season!

shopping tips:

■ Look at money available, a planned budget is ideal.

■ Because Classics need to purchase quality clothing, your motto needs to be "less clothes for more money."

■ Focus on a base color scheme, especially if money is limited for clothing purchases.

■ Focus on ensemble dressing, that is, *finishing* the look from "toes to nose." The Classic coordinates everything from shoes, handbag, and belt to jewelry.

■ Finish or complete *one outfit* at a time. This approach goes with your personality.

■ Always invest in *solid* colors first and refined fabrics are key.

■ Keep an eye on fashion trends, not fads, to stay current and fashionable.

prototypes:

■ Grace Kelly, Nancy Reagan, Lee Remick, Diane Sawyer, Cybill Shepherd

THE CLASSIC

Businesswear
and daywear.

THE DRAMATIC

The Dramatic is expressed in a sophisticated high-fashion look. Some Dramatics go to outrageous extremes with their style. You will immediately visualize this look if you think of Cher. This type of Dramatic is often more trendy and even artsy if they have a sporty Natural bent.

The more sophisticated high-fashion Dramatic has a richer appearance, allowing her to move into some professional settings much more easily than the "trendy" or artsy Dramatic who will usually choose careers in creative fields like fashion or interior design or the arts.

Wherever the sophisticated Dramatic goes, she causes heads to turn. People want to see what she has on and how she put it together. The Dramatic personality is one of mystery, majesty, and inspiration—another reason she turns heads.

The Winter is the most obvious and typical Dramatic because the colors she wears are so vivid and highly contrasted. The other seasons' drama will have less impact. Her choices are daring and full of surprises.

She exerts authority so naturally and her opinions have such great influence that she often becomes the "mouthpiece" or the speaker for her group. She can be, and often is, very direct and demanding, which causes some people to feel intimidated or alienated by her or around her. However, there is a sensitive fragile side that is often hidden by her drama.

It's all or nothing when she entertains. She likes large groups and a lavish array of foods.

She is a risk taker. She's happiest owning her own business. She enjoys being in control.

She is a private person which becomes more apparent as you attempt to get close to her. You will find it difficult because she cannot easily "bare her soul" or share her inner struggles or feelings with others.

Because of a perceived aloofness or brusqueness, she needs to move toward people with kind words of praise, a touch of the hand, or a smile.

As you may have guessed by now, she allows no grass to grow under her feet. She's always moving forward!

body type:

- Height will be in the taller range (5'8" plus).

- Bone structure will be narrow and angular.

- Overall look can be exotic.

THE DRAMATIC

Businesswear and daywear.

facial features:

- Features appear chiseled and angular.

- Some features may have an exotic appearance, such as a prominent nose, high chiseled cheekbones, or angular jawline based on ethnic background.

hairstyle:

- Sleek geometric or asymmetrical styles are best.

- Curly layers or soft shapes diminish drama and can create a "plain Jane" image.

clothing styles:

- Lines should be sleek, long, and *always* straight.

- Styles are high-fashion, and garments are severely tailored.

- Shoulder lines are sharp and often square.

- Necklines have angular shapes and edges.

- Extreme or exotic dress is best for evening.

- The *only* appropriate softness in line is *elongated* draping.

- Ensemble dressing is an important part of the Dramatic sophistication.

fabrics:

- Any fabric choice must hold a defined shape.

- Appropriate choices would be gabardines, failles, stiff brocades, taffetas, linens, etc.

- Patterns are bold and sweeping, abstract, or geometric.

- Head-to-toe dark colors or dark neutrals are also great.

details:

- Flamboyant, lavish, oversized.

- Man-tailored or severely tailored lines are great.

unflattering choices:

- Overdoing a good thing, thus "discounting" the look.

- Delicate, intricate, or small accessories.

THE DRAMATIC

Casualwear.

THE DRAMATIC

Eveningwear.

- Flouncy, frilly, or flowing lines.

- Anything rounded, swirled, or overly draped.

- Overly sheer, lightweight, or extremely rough-textured fabrics.

shopping tips:

- Look at money available; a planned budget is ideal.

- Put the focus on current trends in clothing and accessories. Most of the time, this comes naturally to the Dramatic.

- The greater amount of money will almost always be spent on accessories. This is where the Dramatic's uniqueness lies. Too many Dramatics spend more on their clothes, which diminishes their ability to set themselves apart and keep a rich, sophisticated look.

- The Dramatic can economize on base garments, *never* on accessories, except for "great buys"!

- *Whatever* you choose *must* make a statement.

- Ensemble dressing is also key to your sophistication and richness. You will always finish your look like the Classic but with Dramatic accessorization. You tend to collect accessories.

Note: There are a lot of Dramatic "wannabes" just like there are a lot of Winter "wannabes." Most clothing personalities can use a little drama, but it must be done with care and good taste.

prototypes:

- Cher, Ava Gardner, Barbra Streisand, Diane Carroll, Marlene Dietrich, Joan Crawford

THE ROMANTIC

The Romantic is a "sexy lady" born to be curvy and very feminine. She is the epitome of femininity and sex appeal, even as a teenager. This woman does not have plastic surgery to create her curvaceous figure; her attributes are God given. Obviously, she needs to dress in keeping with her femininity but with good taste and appropriateness or she will look like a "streetwalker." When she enters a room full of people, most of the women present will feel threatened by her sex appeal.

She's a charming, enchanting, and magnetic personality. She can be enormously accommodating and sympathetic with a sweet sensitivity. Because of this she easily suffers hurt. She even

THE ROMANTIC

Casualwear.

possesses an extraordinary human empathy, in a sense able to "walk in someone else's shoes" and feel what they feel. In fact, she can walk into a situation and instinctively have a "feel" for the situation that exists there.

She gives great attention to the sensual elements of taste, smell, touch, and especially to how things look because life must have visual appeal as well as function. Candlelight, music, and floral scents will enhance her environment.

There is an irresistible quality about her which gives her the capability of effecting vast change as long as it's always with indirect attack, not direct. She will never be taken seriously if she plunges ahead with directness. Her force has a manipulative quality to it. With her special abilities almost anything she truly desires seems to come through for her. Her motto is "do what you love and the money will come."

body type:

- Height is average to short, not tall.

- Figure proportions are very shapely, rounded, and soft.

- The bust is always full regardless of weight.

- Hips and buttocks are always rounded with a defined waistline even if heavy.

facial features:

- Features are attractively soft and rounded.

- Eyes are large and flirty.

- There is a natural feminine beauty even without much make-up.

hairstyle:

- Length will be somewhat long to short.

- Style will be softly curled layers if long or feathered around the face if short.

- There should be softness and bounce to any length.

- Romantic styles are never straight, blunt, or stringy.

THE ROMANTIC

Businesswear and daywear.

clothing style:

- Lines are rounded or curved with lots of draping.

- Flowing shapes with a defined waistline are important in dress styles.

- Feminine lines will always be soft, sometimes intricate or even ornate.

- It's important to maintain fluidity from head to toe.

- Waist definition is a must even in jackets or suits.

- *Never* box in this figure.

fabrics:

- Weights should be light to medium.

- Finishes should be rich and luscious.

- Good fabrics for the Romantic are silks, soft wool crepes or wool jersey, sweater knits like angora or cashmere, and suedes or soft leather.

- For evening, velvet, chiffon, and lace are best.

- Prints include oversize florals, polka dots, and feathery shapes.

accessories:

- Jewelry is dainty in detail but lavish in effect.

- Evening looks are ornate.

- Diamonds suit this look especially well.

- Silk scarves and flowers often work well.

- Rarely more than a lavish earring is needed because the garment itself is already finished with accessory details. This could be lavish buttons, metallic or thread embroidery, or stitched-on beading, such as pearls, sequins, or rhinestones.

details:

- Soft intricate, ornate, or feminine details should be used, especially around the face.

- Necklines should be softly draped or curved.

- Shoulders should not be tailored and flat but rounded or curved. Tucks or gathers create softness.

- The waistline is defined, often with feminine or intricate belts.

THE ROMANTIC

Eveningwear.

unflattering choices:

- Clothes that cheapen the appearance.

- Symmetrical shapes and severe silhouettes.

- Tailored, sharp, straight, or horizontal lines.

- Rough textures.

shopping tips:

- Look at funds available; a planned budget is ideal.

- Before you start shopping for clothes, you must *find* your style in the stores or catalogs *first. Boutiques are often a good resource.*

- Focus on spending the most money from the waist up.

- The garment itself, more often a one- or two-piece dress, must express your style. It must *feel* like you. It must have that Romantic visual appeal.

- Your pitfall, because of the desire for that visual appeal or romance in the garment, is that you often choose a correct style but in cheap fabrics. You can not sacrifice quality or you look cheap or "discounted" very quickly. You can not afford to succumb to that temptation.

- Always accessorize to finish the garment's theme.

- Romantics can *economize* on their *accessories* because a lot of inexpensive accessories are produced for this look which utilize pearls first and then rhinestones.

prototypes:

- Liz Taylor, Jaclyn Smith, Rita Hayworth, Sophia Loren, Joan Collins, Donna Mills, Jane Seymour

THE INGENUE

The Ingenue and the Romantic share common natural feminine traits and personality but differ greatly in their physical attributes as the former is the sweet, youthful, innocent portrait of femininity and the latter is the charming "sexy lady." The Ingenue is *not* sexy and alluring but instead has a fresh youthful quality. She is naively feminine. When she enters a room, she brings a special quality of freshness. She is not threatening to other women in her presence, instead her seemingly demure appearance invites people to feel she needs protection and care.

THE INGENUE

Casualwear.

THE INGENUE
Eveningwear.

THE INGENUE
Businesswear
and daywear.

body type:

■ This feminine, small-boned, soft body type is dainty.

■ Regardless of height this frame is often delicate-looking.

■ Figure traits or proportions are gently rounded.

facial features:

■ Cheeks and chin are rounded.

■ Eyes are large and innocent.

■ Features are fine-boned.

■ Coloring tends to be more delicate.

hairstyle:

■ Longer hair should be *softly* curled.

■ Shorter hair should be feathered around the face.

■ The Gibson girl style is very good on the Ingenue.

clothing style:

■ Frocks may have frills, ruffles, and lace.

■ Old-fashioned feminine styles like Laura Ashley, Gunny Sax, or the Victorian styles suit this look.

■ "Granny dresses" in lightweight fabrics and small prints are best worn by the Ingenue.

■ Embroidered detailing is very appropriate.

fabrics:

■ Lightweight, soft woolens, angora, fine silk, fine cotton, crisp cotton, voile, gauze, crocheted knits, or challis are all suitable. More often than not your fabrics have a *crisp* quality.

accessories:

■ Jewelry is small, dainty, and often antique.

■ Feminine florals, ribbons, bows, and cameos are all Ingenue.

unflattering choices:

- Becoming quietus or outdated.

- Soft flowing lines, fabrics, and proportions like the Romantic.

shopping tips:

- Look at available funds; a planned budget is ideal.

- Before shopping, just like the Romantic, you must find stores or catalogs that carry your style; sometimes it's even the junior departments.

- Fabric quality is *not* crucial; you can wear *less* expensive clothes and have a more expansive wardrobe. The exception to this approach would be your professional clothes. They will have a more Ingenue/Classic look.

- Your pitfall is *not* finishing your look, whether it be your shoes, bag, coat, even jewelry.

- As an Ingenue, you can economize on your accessories like the Romantic as there are many similarities.

- The ideal season for you to shop and find your style is Spring or Summer.

prototypes:

- Helen Hayes, Goldie Hawn, Charlene Tilton, Barbara Mandrell

THE NATURAL

Businesswear and daywear.

THE NATURAL

The sporty Natural, more than any other personality, knows who she is from a very young age. She needs comfortable clothes, which is why her clothes are less tailored and more unstructured than the Classic style. Sporty Naturals often choose professions that do not require "professional dress" clothing but rather a uniform or casual clothing. Because she has a preference for informality and less structure, "dressing up" is often a challenge to her. Lack of confidence in her choices for business or professional clothes often cause her to choose safer, traditional Classic styles which tend to look matronly or even boring on her unless she has a Classic side with her Natural personality.

She is *not* an "ensemble dresser" but has a mix-and-match separates style. It is freshly appealing without fuss. Nothing is overdone with her

THE NATURAL

Eveningwear.

because her clothing is functional. This means she can and should choose separate jackets, pants, and skirts of different *textures* and colors to create a youthful, approachable, and fashionable appearance. Her style has a "lived in" feel to it. As she becomes aware of her fashion image, she gains confidence in her ability to make good choices. Shopping, which heretofore was probably a chore, can actually become a tolerable or even pleasant experience. Because of the wonderful natural quality in her appearance, she can look sexy in a T-shirt and boxer shorts, even hiking boots, that would otherwise destroy any other personality's feminine sexuality.

The Natural needs to pay attention to her fabrics. It is best if they are somewhat to very textured in either woven or knitted garments. As she moves into evening clothes, she must search further than most personalities because the manufacturers produce more Romantic or Classic things. Simple elegance is her evening look in brocades, crepes, microfiber jersey knit, velvets, and channel-beading for glamour.

The sporty Natural is a great team player. She's a loyal, faithful friend or employee. With that loyalty comes a very dependable individual because of her sense of responsibility. Every family or organization is blessed if they have this person because she will always be there for you. Material things or how things look are usually not her focus; relationships will receive far more attention. She usually enjoys life to the fullest and so entertaining others has a no "fuss or muss" approach. How the table is set or what is used are secondary in her thinking, and the fact that others know that about her doesn't bother her. These traits will, of course, be modified by the degree of influence from her secondary personality whether it be Ingenue, Romantic, Dramatic, Classic, or even Gamin. In the workplace they are typically work-horses, upbeat and supportive with good insight, able to cut right to the heart of a situation. This all makes for a fun coworker.

body type:

- Height is average to tall.

- Body is strong and sturdy in appearance, whether hips are curvy with a nice waistline or hips are straight with a thicker waist.

- Bone structure is softly angular with broad to average shoulder width.

- Body may be slightly muscular.

facial features:

- Shape of face will be broad (round or square) or long as in oblong.

- Features of face may be uneven or asymmetrical with blunt edges, particularly on broad face. Nose may even be broad and flat.

hairstyle:

- Hairstyle is tousled, loose, and windblown.

- Her style is never "fussy." She will never have an "every hair in place" look.

- Smooth, sleek, blunt cuts should be avoided unless you are half Classic.

clothing style:

- Garments are unstructured; tailoring is simple and soft.

- Garments have no fuss or precise fit.

- Garments are loose and soft for easy mobility.

- Details are minimal.

- Separates should dominate the wardrobe.

- Mix-and-match patterns, textures, and colors.

- Designer sportswear is the look.

fabrics:

- Textures are soft, rough, or nubby.

- Crinkled or wrinkled looks are good.

- Knits will often be jersey, cabled, studded, or nubby.

- Raw silks can be wonderful as well as tweeds, flannels, wool challis, linens, cottons, and denims.

accessories:

- She seldom desires to finish her look with added details. This is typical of most Naturals. If she is making good choices within her style, she does not need to focus on more than a good pair of earrings, a high-quality belt, handbag, and shoes.

unflattering choices:

- Severely man-tailored looks that destroy her femininity.

- Comfort only. She must always remember she can have both comfort and style.

THE NATURAL

Casualwear.

- Sloppy, unkempt appearance, poor grooming principles.

- Use of pearls, which are Romantic or Classic in personality.

shopping tips:

- Look at available funds; a planned budget is ideal.

- If you are a traditional sporty Natural, which is a combination of Classic/Natural, then avoid discount store shopping because you will become frustrated if you don't like to shop. *Most* Naturals were not "born to shop" and usually discount stores don't carry the look.

- Shop department stores, catalogs, or specialty stores like Talbot's. If you are on a tight budget, shop at sale times during the year. Department stores usually have specialty departments for the sporty Natural.

- Discount stores or the cheaper clothing chain stores won't even carry the traditional Natural look because this style is not produced in cheaper fabrics.

- Catalogs that contain traditional sporty Natural styles or Classic/Natural styles are Jos. A. Bank Women, Lands End, Eddie Bauer, Mark, Fore, Strike, and of course, the already mentioned Talbot's.

- The more contemporary sporty Natural styles are found in the "lower end" stores as well as "higher end." This style originated on the West Coast because of the more casual lifestyle there. The fabrics used in many of these clothes are rayon, polyrayon, polycotton, cheaper cotton, polywool, or rayon wool combinations. The quality is often only fair to even poor in low-priced garments. Higher-priced garments contain better quality.

- The more contemporary sporty Natural or Natural/Dramatic will find her look in catalogs like Victoria's Secret, C.W., Pastille, Spiegel, Bloomingdales, Bila, Nordstrom's, etc.

- Focus on *texture* or *prints* instead of the smooth or refined fabrics and solid colors of the Classic.

- Regarding accessories, focus on one good quality handbag, belts, and a pair of good leather shoes. Earrings will finish your look; however, jewelry is rarely your focus.

- Beyond these guidelines, personal taste prevails. You rarely are willing to stretch and risk new looks or try very much jewelry. You like your comfort zone.

prototypes:

- Carol Burnett, Farrah Fawcett, Cheryl Tiegs, Brooke Shields, Jane Fonda, Chris Evert Lloyd, Ali McGraw

THE GAMIN

The Gamin is the most misunderstood of all the personalities. Many Gamins want to be another personality style or even think they are a combination of all others. The reason is twofold. She is a gal of great energy and talent. She's fun but focused. Her look is snappy but chic. She is also petite if she's not combined with Dramatic, Natural, or Classic. She's often subconsciously unwilling to accept her petiteness and does not want to be called cute and yet so often she's adorably cute!

She is not a miniature of any other personality. Her style is related to the Classic more than any other personality. However, the refined fabrics and lines of the Classic change in the Gamin look. She wears *broken, staccato patterns and colors*. They must be *animated* or have *energy* and *movement* in their presentation on the garment. Her personality can not really blossom until she uses this approach to wardrobing.

Her personality is usually spunky, energetic, and in some cases even dazzling. Some people are not quite sure how to take her or even if they want to! She can be vivacious and dynamic. She is a charmer, definitely people-oriented! She loves fun and a good time. Many Gamins take "the party" with them wherever they go.

She's very determined to accomplish her goals. In fact, if you tell her she can't, she will be all the more determined and probably successful as well. Because of her enthusiasm, she's a great cheerleader. She loves the stage because she'll perform, entertain, and have a great time. She'll easily take on or head up a cause if she finds good reason. She'd much rather socialize than domesticate. If a negotiator is needed, she's usually great with words and has the intellect and seriousness of mind to consider all the details and come up with the best possible solution.

THE GAMIN

Businesswear and daywear.

body type:

- Height will be 5'5" and under.

- Build is small to medium.

- Her body can be straight, slim and taut, or chunky and stocky.

- If she is curvy, she will have Romantic with the Gamin.

- If she's very slim and angular, she is likely to be Gamin/Dramatic.

facial features:

- If slim, the features are angular.

- Cheeks and chin can be small and rounded.

- Many have a turned-up nose.

- Face and eyes are usually quite expressive and even animated.

hairstyle:

- Length should be short; cropped in boyish cuts or bobbed at jaw line.

- Layering is an option in short styles.

- Sassiness should be conveyed in her style.

clothing style:

- Lines should be straight and tailored for the slim Gamin.

- The silhouette should be precisely fitted for energy to be conveyed.

- Patterns and colors should be broken or staccato and animated.

- Gamin styles are snappy and chic with lots of crisp contrasted trims, braided trims, or beading.

- Many of her styles are contemporary in feeling.

- Details will always be small, sharp, and eye-catching.

fabrics:

- Colors should be as bold and sassy as the seasonal palette can create.

- Multicolor splashes or caricatures are great.

- Prints should be colorful, animated, and contemporary.

- Fabric texture should be crisp enough to hold defined shape.

- Surfaces are refined or smooth.

- Matte or low-luster finishes of fabric surfaces are best.

- Weights of fabric are light to moderate such as oriental silks, crisp cottons, or wool gabardine.

- Evening fabrics should be sleek, with tailored edges, angular necklines, even asymmetrical hemlines. Crisp metallics and beading are also good.

accessories:

- Jewelry pieces should be scaled to body proportions tending to smaller sizes.

- Jewelry details are crisp, geometric, asymmetric, or irregular and, when garment is casual to dressy casual, even very colorful.

- Style of jewelry will be more Classic with emphasis on a tailored crispness.

- Gamins are the only personality who uses contrasting hosiery colors for a more staccato appearance.

- Dark hosiery should be sheer.

THE GAMIN

Casualwear.

unflattering choices:

- Monochromatic color schemes that sap the energy from the look.

- Neutrals, unless merely accessories.

- Flowering, soft fabrics that drape or hang.

- Oversized or unstructured shapes.

- Rough textures.

- Sheer, delicate fabrics.

- Frilly, flimsy blouses.

- Antique, artisan, or intricate jewelry designs.

shopping tips:

- Look at available funds; a budget is ideal.

- Your focus will usually be petite sizing.

- You are a mix-and-match dresser, somewhat like the Natural but with the smoother, refined fabrics of the Classic.

- Avoid any monochromatic dressing or garments unless you are combined with another personality.

- Choose garments that utilize the artful breaking up of color or staccato coloring.

- Coordinate minimally two or three colors into your garment.

- Remember one color needs to dominate as a foundation color.

- Accessorize with the dominant color.

prototypes:

- Sandy Duncan, Bonnie Franklin, Karen Valentine, Sally Fields, Marie Osmond, Julie Andrews, Leslie Caron, Carol Channing

COMBINATION CLOTHING PERSONALITIES

Combination personalities exist where the dominant personality is determined by physical structure/body type, hair type and style preferences, along with facial features. The secondary personality is determined by physical features not aligned with your dominant personality and also by your personality traits.

CLASSIC COMBINATIONS

The Classic/Natural, the Classic/Ingenue, the Classic/Dramatic.

EXAMPLES OF WORKABLE COMBINATIONS:

Classic/Dramatic is predominantly Classic because of physical characteristics that are balanced and symmetrical. The Dramatic influence may come in with height over 5'7" or elongated legs, feet, and hands. The personality traits may be very dramatic in nature. She will always focus on the style of the garment, with a strong Classic influence. She begins to express her drama through her choice of accessories. She will utilize more bold pieces to finish her look than a Classic would. She's attracted to accessories—jewelry, belts, scarves, handbags, shoes, etc.

Classic/Romantic eliminates any *tailored traits,* such as notched collars or tailored set-in sleeves. She finishes her Classic look with romantic touches.

Classic/Natural is prone to ensemble dressing with soft tailored influences in cut and style. Plaids, houndstooth, and tweeds will attract her. She is not a separates dresser.

Dramatic/Classic is predominately Dramatic because she is tall and slender, with unusual angular facial features. She dresses in the higher fashion versions of a Classic-elegant look that has obvious Dramatic flares. Her look is more frequently found in higher-priced garments. These will be found in specialty departments or shops. She will feel dowdy and boring in a Classic garment until it is highly accessorized.

Dramatic/Romantic averages 5'4" to 5'8" in height with such feminine features as a pretty face, hands, and feet. She uses high-fashion looks with a lot of detailing on the garment, such as elaborate buttons, beads, imitation gem stones, braiding, and color accents.

Dramatic/Natural will always be tall. She is attracted to more contemporary designs and lines. Key terms would be oversized, elongated, novelty textures, and large geometric patterns. She will utilize chunky bold jewelry, shoes, boots, etc. in her looks. She expresses her Dramatic side in ensemble dressing, not mix-and-match.

Romantic/Classic is predominately Romantic because of her curvy figure and feminine features. She will choose more curved and fitted silhouettes instead of Classic boxy styles. However the fabrics and styles will have a great deal of Classic influence. There is a conservative side to her personality that inhibits her freedom to be 100% Romantic. Unlike the true Romantic, she has the ability, because of her Classic side, to avoid looks that cheapen her image.

DRAMATIC COMBINATIONS

The Dramatic/Romantic, the Dramatic/Natural.

ROMANTIC COMBINATIONS

The Romantic/Dramatic, the Romantic/Classic.

Ingenue/Classic is average in height. She does not have an innocent look of the true Ingenue. But she has a youthful feminine figure and soft feminine facial features. For business wear, she chooses more Classic influences with soft feminine features, such as floral patterns or touches of lace. In casual wear, she chooses Ingenue looks.

Natural/Classic is predominately Natural because of her sturdy body build, and she may have an elongated or wide face. Her hairstyle may be more carefree, less controlled, but not "wash and go." When dressing for business, she chooses Classic styles. When dressing casually, she chooses sporty Natural styles. Because she limits her accessories, she expresses her look through fabric textures.

Natural/Ingenue is not a sturdy body type. She has a softly curved or straighter build. Regardless of height, she has a tendency to appear tall. She uses a lot of textured fabrics with feminine features on the garment. She has a sporty Natural face shape but more feminine eyes.

Natural/Romantic has curvy body features. She gravitates to country-western influences, such as nipped in waists, crisp ruffles, and fitted jeans with studs. She has the greatest challenge expressing her combo-personality style in business wear. She will need to go softly Natural or softly feminine.

Gamin/Classic personality is determined by her height, 5'4" to 5'5", and her Gamin personality traits. She's more Classic in appearance but more Gamin in temperament. For her Gamin personality, she must add some Gamin staccato color splashes and avoid too much ensemble dressing like the Classic. Her lines will be more Classic and her use of color more Gamin.

Gamin/Dramatic is determined by a slender more angular body and facial features, yet shorter in height. Her hairstyle will be more geometric or asymmetrical in style. Whatever she does in high-style or high-fashion looks, she must keep her garments defined to her shape—not loose or oversized.

Gamin/Romantic is petite with curvy, rounded features. She wears animated and staccato-shaped garments. Her fabrics are crisp and formed, hugging the body. She uses an abundance of prints to create excitement. Her garments have a sexy, feminine influence.

Gamin/Ingenue is petite and delicate with small-boned features. Her personality is more reserved. She uses medium- to lighter-weight fabrics, regardless of season, and her garments have soft, feminine details, such as lace, bows, and tiny floral prints. Because the Ingenue's combination is more petite, she will give up elongated looks for more fitted styles.

Gamin/Natural is a Natural body type in miniature with a stocky build. She must avoid the Natural's unstructured garment styles and keep her mix-and-match garments crisp, staccato, and body-contoured. She uses textured fabrics of the Natural but avoids the loose, oversized garments. She looks good in pictorial sweaters, stitched-down pleated skirts, cropped blazers, and cotton blouses.

NOTES

CHAPTER FOUR

WHAT SHOULD
I DO WITH MY HAIR?

I can understand how any woman could be frustrated with her hair. When I was younger, mine caused me a great deal of distress at times. I grew up in the '50s, and we didn't have blow dryers, curling irons, mousse, gels, or any of the great styling techniques we have today. My hair is very fine, and as a result, I literally spent hours trying to make it look good. Based on that experience, I am very aware of how important a good hairstyle is to a woman's self-image. Even the Bible states that a woman's hair is her crowning glory.

Women need encouragement and direction with their hairstyles. It's crucial to have a good cut that you can manage by yourself. As a consultant, I have learned everything I can about hairstyle and color because I believe it is of utmost importance to my clients and students.

The most common question I get from women is "How do I find a good hairstylist?" It's not easy, but you have to persist. First, look at the stylist's hairstyle. Is it flattering and current? Do her clients all look the same, or does she take the time to discuss the client's face shape, profile, and hair texture? The stylist should handle your hair, play with it, move it to see where your cowlicks and thin spots are located.

Always ask to see photos of styles that are suggested to you. Do you like any of them? Find out how difficult or easy the suggested style is to maintain. If you have no skill or time to duplicate the suggested style, then make sure that you tell your stylist. Many of the techniques used to create style today are really not difficult to learn if you ask for help.

When my stylist changes my style, I use a hand mirror to watch the back as well as the front while she is blow drying and curling my hair. It's important to see how she "picks" or "fingers" your hair into its shape. It is in the stylist's best interest to give you all the help possible because if you look good, your stylist looks good.

Another way to find a good stylist is to look at hair styles when you are in public. It is a compliment to any woman to be stopped and asked where she has her hair done.

A good stylist will update her training at least once a year. She must keep abreast of changing styles and techniques for cutting hair. However, all stylists in a particular salon are not necessarily equally skilled or current in their techniques of styling or coloring hair. Read the magazines and be aware of how styles are changing. Women date themselves very quickly by wearing an out-of-date hairstyle.

CONSIDER YOUR FACE SHAPE

When choosing a hair style among those recommended, your face shape is the first consideration. The perfect face shape is oval; those of us who do not have oval faces strive to achieve the illusion with a flattering hairstyle.

The most important feature of any hairstyle is that it balances or offsets any imbalance in the face. For example, if you have a long face, then you must add width, not more length, to the face. If you have a triangular or pear-shaped face, then you must add fullness from the eyes up to balance the lower, wider part of your face.

You should not repeat your face shape with your hairstyle. No rounded looks on the round face or square looks on the square face, etc. Just apply good principles of balance, based on the shape of your head, your profile, and your head set. A good stylist will look at these features and discuss them with you.

When considering the face shape, the position and prominence of the facial bones are primary. There are basically seven face shapes: the oval, oblong, diamond, heart shape, pear shape, round, and square.

The face is divided into three sections: forehead to brow, brow to end of nose, and end of nose to bottom of chin. When choosing a good hairstyle, you will be working to create the balance of those facial sections.

Oval face

Oblong-shaped face

Diamond-shaped face

Heart-shaped face

Pear-shaped face

Round face

Square face

FLATTERING HAIRSTYLES

For different face shapes

The **oval face** can wear almost any style. As it ages, however, it should avoid any style that lengthens the face as the face is one and a half times longer than the width across the brow area. The chin is slightly narrower than the brow section.

The **oblong face** appears longer than the oval and will often have hollow cheeks. The jawbone and cheekbone are equal in width. The goal is to make the face appear shorter so you add width to the style and cover some of the forehead.

The **diamond-shaped face** has a narrow forehead with greater width at the cheekbone and more narrow at the chin. The goal is to increase width and fullness at the jawline and forehead. Avoid styles that lift out or away from the cheekbone area.

The **heart-shaped face** has a wider brow and cheekbone. The jawline dramatically narrows. The goal is to reduce the width of the forehead and add fullness and width at the jawline and chin.

The **pear-shaped face** has a narrow forehead and wide jawline. The goal is to create the illusion of width at the forehead. Either short or longer hairstyles are best, not midlength.

The **round face** is wider than two-thirds of its length. The cheek-bones are wider than the brow bone or jawline. The goal here is to create the illusion of length. Use asymmetrical parts and styles. Avoid horizontal lines.

The **square face** is straight along the sides of the face and has a square jawline created by an equal width at the brow bone, cheekbone, and jawline. The width of the face is noticeably wider than two-thirds of its length. The goal is to lengthen the face. Hair length should fall below the jawline. Never use horizontal lines in hairstyle as with the round face. Asymmetrical styles are the best.

Here are some other very important considerations: If you are plump with a short- or no-neck appearance, avoid hairstyles that add fullness to the back of the neck. Build height on top.

If you have a prominent nose, never sweep the hair back from the face. Move it forward onto the face. When the chin recedes as well, move bangs onto the forehead and keep the hair close to the nape of the neck because the forehead often recedes giving a convex profile.

On the other hand, if the profile is concave with a prominent chin, the hair should move softly upward from the nape of the neck.

To minimize a broad flat nose which often widens the face, draw the hair away from the face. If appropriate also use a center part.

HAIRSTYLES FOR THE CLASSIC

CONSIDER YOUR CLOTHING PERSONALITY

In any hair style decision, clothing person-ality must be considered. The following illustrations give you some of the looks that are appropriate to each of the follow-ing groups:

HAIRSTYLES FOR THE ROMANTIC

HAIRSTYLES FOR THE INGENUE

HAIRSTYLES FOR THE DRAMATIC

HAIRSTYLES FOR THE NATURAL

Remember not to choose clothing personality on the basis of the hairstyle you like but on the basis of what clothing personality *flatters* your body and facial characteristics.

The Classic hairstyle is symmetrical in form. Any length above the shoulder is appropriate as long as it is controlled in appearance. The Classic bob or page boy is great as well as shorter lengths. It is never tousled or stringy.

The Romantic and Ingenue hairstyles may be "textured," layered and softly curled with fullness. If pulled off the face, then wispy tendrils falling around the face and neck are very attractive. Any length is fine as long as it is soft and curly. It should not be a wash-and-go curly look.

The Dramatic hairstyles make definite statements. They are usually precision geometric cuts with or without bangs. Asymmetrical styles are often used. Most styles are controlled, sometimes pulled back or high on the head giving a very sleek appearance. Lengths are either extremely long or short. They are never layered or softly curled.

Sporty Natural styles are uncontrolled, more tousled and "wash and wear" in appearance. Carefree and low-maintenance styles are key to this look.

Gamin styles are controlled to somewhat looser in appearance. Their look is often boyishly bobbed or cropped in short layers. The key objective here is "perky" or "sassy."

CONSIDER THE STYLIST'S EXPERTISE

The right stylist, however, is not necessarily the best colorist. In the very finest salons, whether in Beverly Hills or New York City, you may visit one person for your hairstyle and another for your color, and still another for a perm. Any beautician who has been licensed by her state has had to pass a test in all three of these areas, but that is still not a guarantee that she is talented in all three. I find that often a gifted stylist, one who is creative and

understands proportion and balance, is not able to correctly translate these gifts into the color area; she may tend to be too creative with color.

Creating warm hair color tones is much easier than creating good cool/ash tones—an honest beautician will tell you that. Depending on porosity and texture of the hair, it will lift color at different rates. What works for one situation will not for the next. Whether you like it or not, the first time someone colors your hair, you are often a "guinea pig," depending on the type of hair you have. Give the stylist the opportunity to perfect your color. It may take a couple appointments to achieve your desired color.

If you find a good stylist, it's worth driving 100 miles once a month to receive her services. Don't settle for mediocre, settle only for the best!

HAIRSTYLES FOR
THE GAMIN

CONSIDER THE CONDITIONS THAT ALTER HAIR COLOR

There are several things that can affect or change your natural hair color depending on the condition and type of hair you have. Sometimes these influences occur so gradually and subtly that you lose track of your natural hair color. You really need to examine new hair growth to determine whether your true color base is cool or warm. Based on that decision you then have direction for what your true hair color range should be.

Hair color changes may result from:

- permanent hair color treatment
- semipermanent hair color application
- frosting, glazing, highlighting
- sun exposure
- permanents
- straightening

- henna shampoos
- chlorinated pools
- well water (rural areas)
- medication
- pregnancy

You need to tell your color consultant if any of these conditions or subtle changes have influenced your hair color.

NOTES

NOTES

CHAPTER FIVE

HOW DO I FINISH MY LOOK?

*I*t has been said that, "Accessories are the leading symbols of a woman's true personality." If this is true, then each of us should start our image development by taking inventory of our accessories. Accessories are anything that is worn other than the garment itself. This means that even your nail color is an accessory. For some of you this inventory would take about 15 minutes, but others of you would need to spend three to four hours, maybe more! Finally our accessories should be an expression of our personal style and personality. Anything you choose as an accessory waist down is a *finishing* point or feature. It should never lead the eye to that area. Anything you choose as an accessory waist up is a *focal* point. This will lead the eye appropriately to the face.

THE FUNCTIONS OF ACCESSORIES

■ They make an outfit look complete or finished. This is definitely a confidence builder.

■ They give visual appeal to plain lines and neutral colors.

■ They create the mood of the outfit if it does not already have one "built-in."

■ They can change the mood of an outfit.

■ They can give a variety of looks to a single outfit.

GUIDELINES FOR CHOOSING ACCESSORIES

- They should be an expression of your own personal style or clothing personality.

- They should feel and look right on you. This means you must feel comfortable wearing them, and their size and proportion should be scaled to your body and clothing.

- They should be colors from your personal color palette. Gold is a metallic color that can be worn by cool skins *if* they do not have silver or white or salt and pepper hair color. Use in place of silver only if the garment is already trimmed in gold.

- They should be complimentary to the color of your outfit.

- They should draw attention away from any figure challenges. For example, flashy bracelets draw attention to the hip area. Long necklaces draw attention away from the chin and neck, but draw attention to the bustline. Short or small chain necklaces make the shoulders appear broader, etc.

- They should create only one focal point. This means as you look at yourself in the mirror, your eyes should be drawn to only one area, not bounce from one to another.

- Your accessory (accent) color should be repeated at least once, two or three times maximum, almost always from the waist up.

- Never mix dressy garments with casual accessories and vice versa.

- Some garments make a statement in themselves, and they need very few accessories. Many times a pair of earrings will finish the look beautifully.

Having considered the functions and guidelines for accessorizing, let's consider the first area of application.

SHOES

- The taller you are, the higher heel you can wear. If you are 5'3" or shorter, do not wear heels higher than 2" to 2 $\frac{1}{2}$". Otherwise, you will look like you are walking on your tiptoes.

- Your shoes should be the same color value as your hemline or darker. The exception is in casualwear. If in doubt, wear a neutral color.

■ When putting together an outfit, start with the shoes. The reason for this is that the clothing and the leather industries have not collaborated in their selection of colors. For example, you may find that navy in the leathers will be the Summer or Autumn shades, but the garment may be in the Winter shade. This obviously creates some difficulty in your coordination attempts. It is a good idea to buy two pairs of shoes to finish an outfit.

■ The classic pump is the most versatile dress shoe. It may have closed or open toes, or be slingback.

■ If you have large legs, avoid straps across the instep of the foot or ankle, wider heels, and round or square toes. These styles enlarge legs and widen the foot.

■ Strappy high-heeled shoes are usually dressy and feminine. They are not appropriate with suits or tailored dresses.

■ Stacked heels with closed toes are strictly sporty, and they do not go with dressy clothes.

■ Clunky shoes are not flattering to any leg size. Be careful when this trend is in. Only the Natural/Dramatic or Dramatic can successfully wear this look.

Two final comments regarding shoes: Women have a tendency not to stay current with heel styles. If your heel style is not shaped like the current classic pumps, you will date your appearance immediately. Shoes must be kept polished; toe tips and heels must be refurbished as needed.

■ shoe styles

business:	casual:	dressy:
pumps	loafers	strappy heels
spectators	flat sandals	silk or brocade
slingbacks	espadrilles	metallic
T-straps	huaraches	Lucite
	sneakers	jeweled
	moccasins	
	Western boots	
	clogs or slides	

SHOE LEATHERS

Calfskin: A standard shoe leather that is good year-round. It is appropriate for daywear, sportswear, or casualwear. The heavier the leather, the sportier it is.

Kidskin: This is good for day or evening, especially for dresses in lightweight fabrics.

Suede: This is good for day to evening, casual or dressy, and fall or winter (it needs weighty fabrics). When worn in the spring, it must be with gabardine or challis because of its need for weighty fabrics. When suede shoes are worn, accessories must also be suede. It is the least durable of all leathers because it is fragile and sensitive. When driving a car, it is wise to wear a different pair of shoes to protect the heels from looking worn.

Patent: This is good for daytime and is best for spring through fall. It can be worn year-round in warm climates. It is appropriate with lightweight fabrics like silks, linens, rayons, or cottons. It is not considered an evening shoe unless it's worn in a slipper-style; then it can also be worn all year.

Fabric: High-luster fabrics, like satin, jeweled, or faille shoes, are appropriate for after five. The low-luster fabrics, like canvas, are for daywear.

Reptile: Snake and eel skin shoes are good for elegant daytime wear, dress or casual chic. The snakeskin can move into evening if desired.

Metallics: Metallic leathers are a great neutral option for any clothing personality. They are appropriate all year, daytime or evening. The finish for daytime pumps should be matte. High luster or matte are fine for evening wear. Some metallics are pearlized which neutralizes and softens the color. When light or bright garment colors are accessorized or trimmed in a metallic silver or gold, the same metallic can be worn in the shoe color. Some deeper and more saturated garment colors will need a pewter or gunmetal shoe shade. Silver, which is the lightest metallic and can look almost white from a distance, *must* be used with a light color when dressing up to prevent attention from being drawn to the feet first.

The pewter or gunmetal metallics could be acceptable in some professional situations if they are not conservative businesses. The shiny gold or silver metallics are fine for daytime when they are used for *casual* footwear only.

HOSIERY

- Hosiery is the finishing touch, not a focal point.

- Hosiery needs to be in the same color base as the garment worn. Avoid warm hosiery colors with cool colors in clothing.

- Colored hosiery may either match the garment or the accessory/accent color. If the hose match the color of the dress or skirt, they add the illusion of height and slimness, particularly in the basic or neutral colors.

- If the hosiery color matches the accessory/accent color, it should *not* outshine the garment color.

- If textured hose are desired, then the texture must balance with the texture of the fabric worn; lightweight texture belongs with delicate fabric and heavy texture with heavy fabrics.

- The best fitting hose come in the tube-style.

- The most durable hose are the control-top, in any brand.

- Lycra increases the durability of any type hosiery.

HANDBAGS

- Handbags should always be "tried on."

- The style of the handbag should be compatible with the clothes worn—sporty with sporty; romantic with romantic, etc. The Classic carries a softly structured bag, such as a quilted Chanel style with gold chain woven with leather ribbon. The Dramatic carries a very structured geometric style, such as triangularly shaped bag. The Natural carries a "status" bag, such as Louis Vuitton, Liz Claiborne, or Gucci bag. The Romantic carries softly gathered leathers that have feminine details. The Ingenue has a similar bag style—soft leather is the key. Gamins choose similar styles to the Classic.

- It should be the same color value as the shoes worn or lighter, and it should harmonize with the outfit colors.

- The size of the handbag should fit between the pelvic bones when held against the front of the body.

- The shoulder bag should never fall at the widest part of the hips but at a narrower point above. Shoulder bags belong with pants or a tailored straight-line suit, otherwise tuck the strap inside the purse.

- Tapestry handbags are for casual use, not for dressy occasions. They are usually trimmed with natural leather or wood and belong to the Natural category.

BELTS

Belts add a great finishing look and can be worn with almost any outfit. No wardrobe is complete without a wide selection of belts. Everyone can wear them, but we can't all wear them in the same way. You must remember the principles of good proportions.

- The best size belt for your waist buckles in the middle hole.

- Square, rectangle, or geometric buckles are best with tailored garments.

- The smooth, curved, oval, or shell buckles compliment the soft, curved body and detail lines.

- The safest width is $1\frac{1}{2}$".

- The color, leather, and style must be compatible with the other leather accessories.

- Cinch belts should be worn only by small to average busts, not large.

- Check discount stores for good buys on better leather belts.

- Women with large hips should never wear narrow or skinny belts. The width should be at least 1", and the belt should have a narrow buckle for a focal point. This creates the illusion of a smaller waist.

- Stay abreast of the current looks as you can update last season's garment with a current belt style.

Note: A good basic belt NEVER goes out of style.

SCARVES

Scarves are great items to finish a look. They may frame the face and neck, adorn the waist, or wrap the head. They never go out of style. They have become increasingly popular because accessories are a bigger item on the fashion scene than ever before. Because clothing is so expensive, scarves and other accessories that can change the look of a garment are a great alternative to buying a new outfit.

■ Scarves can pull contrasting color separates together.

■ Silk scarves are printed in florals, stripes, polka dots, geometrics, or abstracts.

■ Florals are best with more feminine dresses or blouses.

■ Stripes, geometrics, or abstracts are best with tailored clothes that reflect the Classic, Dramatic, or Natural personality.

■ Wool challis scarves are worn primarily with wools or weighty fabrics.

■ The way the scarf is tied should be compatible with the style of the individual outfit. For example, an ascot style should be worn with a traditional Classic/Natural blouse and blazer-style jacket. The "fluffier" style scarves belong with dressmaker-style suits or dresses.

JEWELRY

Remember, there is a fine line between classy and brassy, meaning that you can overdo it with jewelry. Most women, however, do not use enough jewelry. The reason is that most are not sure what to do with it; the following principles will help.

Note: Always apply your perfume before putting on your jewelry to prevent damaging it.

■ The size of jewelry worn should be scaled to the bone structure of the face and body. A large woman should wear large jewelry because dainty jewelry tends to look lost. REMEMBER THE PRINCIPLES OF BALANCE.

■ Oversized garments call for oversized jewelry. This is seen in the Dramatic style especially.

■ Jewelry application begins with the face first, neck second, and wrist third. A scarf may be substituted for a necklace or used in conjunction with it.

- Brushed fine metals can be dressier than highly polished ones, especially in costume jewelry.

- Jewelry metal colors may be mixed; for example, silver with gold. Metallic colors can look elegant on pastels or dazzling on darks.

- The style of jewelry must suit the style of the garment. Pearls, for instance, can be very classic or they can create a feminine Victorian or romantic look, depending on the styling and the mix-with-metal design.

- Sporty clothing and heavier textures require either simple or chunky natural jewelry. Romantic, feminine clothing requires feminine, more delicate accessories, as in fine jewelry.

- If wearing a pin and a necklace together, you must wear the pin on a jacket or outside layer and the necklace on the dress or blouse.

- You can wear clusters of pins on lapels. These pins could be earrings, which can also be used as shoe clips and scarf pins.

- Jewelry pieces do not have to match, but they should blend nicely. For instance, wearing a multiple of Chanel-inspired necklaces (of pearls and gold chains) together can be very rich in appearance along with pearl and gold earrings.

- Any piece of jewelry should be a perfect partner to several garments in your closet.

- A pin the size of a silver dollar or larger should be worn at the jawline level, not at the bustline area. Contrary to popular opinion, it does not have to be placed on the lapel. It can be half-on and half-off or on the garment entirely. Small clusters of pins can be worn on the lapel.

- Keep the pin in "proportion to scale"—the larger the body frame, the larger the pin; the larger the print or pattern or the heavier the fabric texture, the larger the pin and vice versa. Cluster 2 or 3 larger pins for a more dramatic effect.

- Romantics wear necklaces more than any other personality, especially on the skin at the base of the neck or somewhat lower.

CLUSTER OF PINS

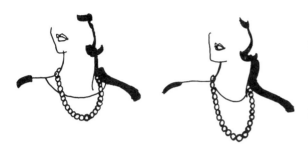

■ Necklace lengths are important to consider. If the neckline is collarless and open, do not wear a necklace that crosses bare skin onto the garment.

■ A necklace never ends at the bustline. If you are average- to small-busted, the necklace may fall below the bustline. If you are full-busted the necklace should end above the bustline.

NECKLACES AND NECKLINES

Unflattering, flattering

NECKLACES AND BUSTLINES

Full-busted imbalance,

full-busted balance,

small- to average-busted

balance.

HATS

Even though very few women wear hats today, the fashion industry has not given up designing and manufacturing them. They add a wonderful dimension to many looks and certainly add a mysterious quality when worn correctly. It is usually the Dramatic, the Ingenue, or the Romantic who wears them for a fashion statement. Classics are too concerned about damaging their hairstyle, and the Natural does not usually even think of wearing one unless it would be for functional purposes.

Hats never go out of style, although they may be more in style at some time than others. Like anything else, hat styles come and go. So make sure the hat stuck away in your closet is not out of style before you wear it. The following principles should be considered when choosing a particular hat to wear or purchase.

- The brim of the hat should be no wider than the shoulders. The taller you are the bigger hat you can wear.

- The crown of the hat should equal the width of your temples.

- Most hats should be worn forward (pulled firmly onto the head) with the crown opening covering a portion of the forehead. It should appear to meet the eyebrows. Many of them should also be tilted on a slight angle. These are the only ways a hat can be fashionable.

- Straw hats go with lightweight fabrics like cottons, chiffons, linens, etc. Seasonally, they are worn in the spring or summer.

- Flannels and felts go with wools or suedes. Seasonally they are worn in the fall and winter.

- If the hat and clothes are the same color, the hat must have a great shape or the clothes must be sharp and fashionable, otherwise the look will be boring.

- With dark colors, choose a bright contrasting trim on the hat and pick this up as your accent color.

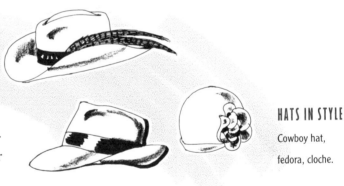

HATS IN STYLE

Cowboy hat, fedora, cloche.

- With pastel colors in clothes, choose a pastel in your hat selection that matches an accent color in another shade. Of course, you need to pick up this accent color in your other accessories.

- Make sure the hat you choose compliments your face, face shape, and profile.

- Don't wear a hat unless you feel confident in your choice and in the look as a hat will draw attention to yourself.

- You should keep your hat on when attending an event. So your choice must be appropriate in size and dressiness.

- Evening/formal hats are always smaller in size and more ornate in trim.

- Your cosmetic application can be a bit bolder when wearing a hat.

- It's best to build the outfit and other accessories around the hat for the greatest effect. Buying the hat last may not always produce the results you want.

- Don't overdo the jewelry at the neck and ears with a hat unless you are a Dramatic.

■ hat personality

natural:	classic:	dramatic:	romantic:
felt fedora	pillbox	anything unusual or extreme in style	soft, floppy brimmed hats
beret or tam	wide-brimmed fedora	deep cloche	pillbox with flowers
boater (gondolier)	picture hats	turban	skullcap with flowers
large, textured straw hats		wide, deep pillbox	anything with flowers, bows, or sparkles
simple cloche (soft crowned hat in a bell shape with a small brim)		flat crown and brim	
deerstalker (Sherlock Holmes)		skullcap with stiffened net brim and bow	
cowboy hat			
fisherman's hat			

EYEWEAR

Every woman who wears glasses at least 50% of the time should have at least two pairs of frames. It is not considered strange or unusual to change clothes 2 or 3 times a day, yet women never think of having more than one pair of glasses. One pair of glasses can be for casualwear and one pair for dress-up.

Choose frames on the basis of facial proportion and coloring.

- The frame should be opposite the face shape:

    – round frames for the square face,

    – square frames for the round face, and

    – almond shape for the pear-shaped face.

- Frames should follow the brow line at the same level unless the current style is oversize or undersize. If a standard size frame is worn and it sets below the brow, it gives the appearance of two sets of brows or a surprised expression. Your optician should make an adjustment to your frame if this happens.

- Frames should be no wider than the widest part of the face.

- Lens height should be equal above and below the eye or the iris should set in the center of the lens. If the lens sets down too low on the face, it destroys the effect of your blush and causes the face to droop.

- Frames that slant or curve upward on the outer edges *lift* your features.

- Avoid frames that slant or point downward on the outside edge.

- Frames should work with the body proportions. For example: small, delicate features with a thin neck and body need a lightweight frame.

- Sunglasses should be a slightly larger version of the regular glass frames.

- See your swatchbook for the best frame colors for your skin tone and hair color.

- Watch frame style trends. Don't date yourself with out-of-style frame, lens size, or stem placement. Use the following chart as your guideline to good frame selection.

WHICH EYEGLASS FRAMES GO BEST WITH MY FACE?

Face Shape–Eyewear Selection Chart

Adapted from Eyewear Ideas, *published by An Enhance-Her Publication*

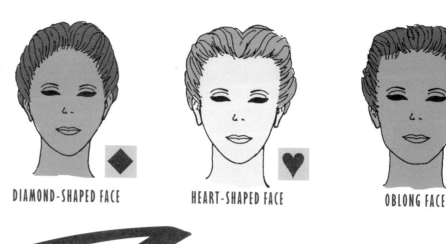

DIAMOND-SHAPED FACE HEART-SHAPED FACE OBLONG FACE

DIRECTIONS: Eyewear should compliment your facial features—your eyes, nose, and face shape. Look at the seven face shapes to determine your own face shape and the symbol to the right that goes with it. Now find the colored symbols that match your face shape on the chart below. The frames above your matching symbol are the frame shapes best suited to your face.

Remember the frames should never wear your face, your face should wear the frame.

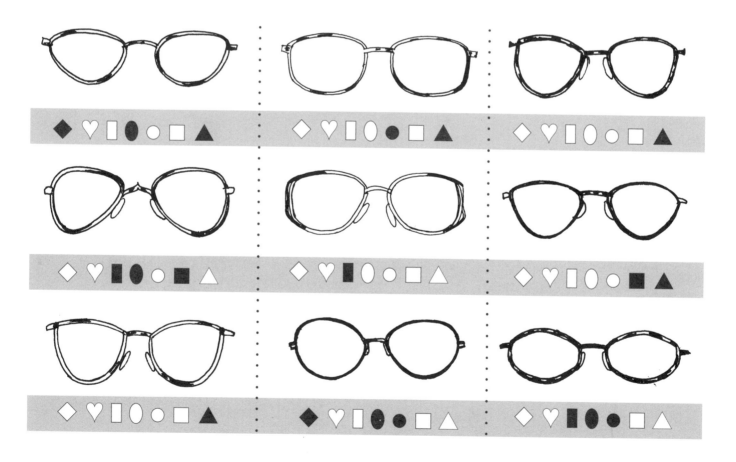

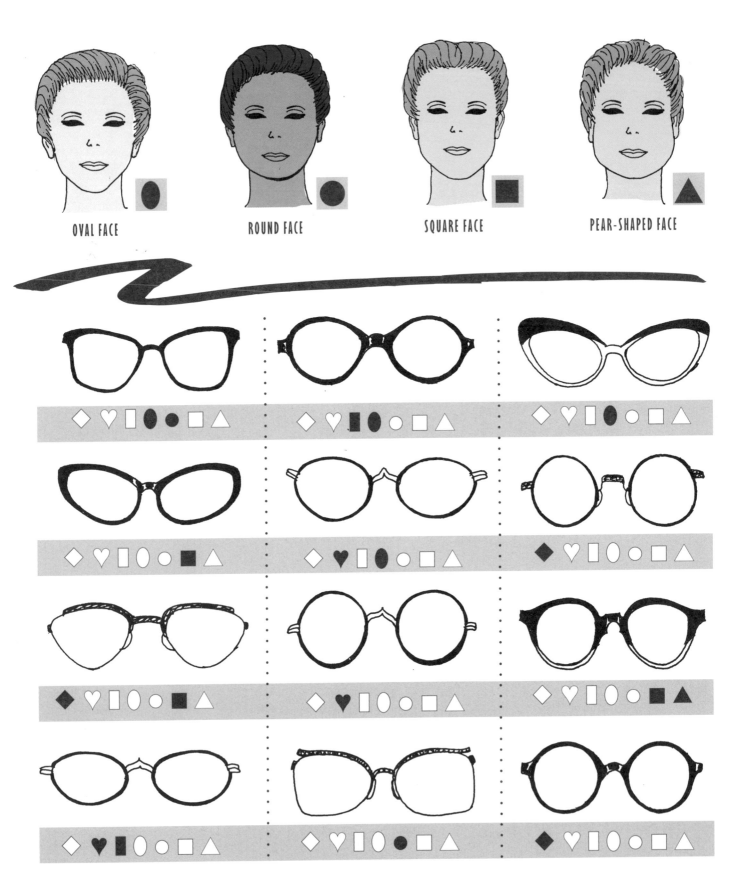

OVAL FACE

ROUND FACE

SQUARE FACE

PEAR-SHAPED FACE

NOTES

NOTES

CHAPTER SIX

IS FABRIC COMPATIBILITY IMPORTANT?

There are three areas in which appropriate fabrics and their compatibility are important in creating a "total look." They are as follows:

- The texture and weight of the fabric must compliment your figure type and personal style.

- The fabrics of each garment piece in your outfit should be compatible with one another.

- The fabrics in your accessories, such as scarves, shoes, hairbows, etc., should be compatible with other garment fabrics you are wearing.

FABRIC TEXTURE AND WEIGHT

Both the fabric weight and the weight of your body play a strong role in your fabric choices. Whether you are at an average weight or 30 pounds overweight with a curvy figure, fabrics that are crisp or stiff, man-tailored in appearance, or heavily textured will not compliment your curves. They will only enlarge your appearance and destroy your natural femininity. Your best fabrics are soft; they drape well and are not too bulky. These include silks, soft wool crepes, jerseys, rayon crepes, challis, and cotton knits or soft weaves.

Straight figures are most complimented by flat, crisp man-tailored fabrics like wool gabardine, sharkskin, linen, and crisp cottons like poplin and trigger cloth. Softly curved or softly straight figures look

best in fabrics that are neither too crisp or too drapey. These people have more flexibility in their choices than either of the other extremes.

The patterns or prints on the various fabric weights and weaves should also be considered. These can either compliment the body or destroy the desired look. Generally speaking, geometric or angular patterns are best on crisp fabrics with tailored lines, whereas floral or free-flowing patterns are best on soft fabrics with curved, feminine lines. Abstract patterns may have a soft appearance, a sharp dramatic look, or various ethnic expressions. This is where clothing style and personality interplays with fabric and line.

GARMENT CHOICES AND FABRIC COMPATIBILITY

As you consider your new clothing purchases, 50% of them should be in fabrics that are wearable year-round. This consideration includes the climate factor as well as fashionableness. The following fabrics would accommodate both cold and warm temperatures:

- raw silk for dresses, jumpsuits, suits, coats, pants

- silk crepe de chine, broadcloth or tissue faille for dresses, blouses, scarves

- cotton knits or sweaters for casual to semicasual

- wool or rayon gabardine for business daywear

- rayon silk blends for business daywear

- rayon crepe for daywear

The number one cardinal rule with fabric mixes is "never combine casual fabrics with dressy fabrics." A good example would be never mix a soft cotton knit dress with a linen-textured silk jacket. The dress is too casual a fabric for the dressier jacket. Many times a good clue will be the dressiness of the style in one versus the casualness of the other. Another good example is the inappropriateness of a washable silk blouse with a cotton poplin pant or skirt.

MAKING WISE DECISIONS

Retail clerks in the better stores can often be of help but don't always depend on them. In many of the youth-oriented stores, they mix anything—good taste or not. Many times they seek to make an extreme statement rather than a good fashion statement. This is where you see dressy nylon lace combined with a casual crinkle cotton, etc. It is perfectly acceptable for young students but not in the more serious business/social environments. When young people grow up wearing that type of look, they have a more difficult time choosing the "right" clothes when they get out in the business world.

The John T. Malloy image is certainly no longer the norm in the business world, especially not in the '90s. There is definitely more emphasis on personal style and good taste than on asexual business images.

Coming back more specifically to fabric compatibility, blouse fabrics that mix well with wool and wool blends are silks, cotton blends, polyester or polyester blends, or silk and wool blends. Blouse fabrics that mix well with linen, raw silks, or cottons include lightweight linen or ramie, rayon, cotton, and some silks or silk looks in polyester. Keep the weights and lusters balanced in mixing your fabrics, whether the same or contrasting.

Wintertime suit fabrics include the various wool weaves (flannels, tweeds, crepes, or gabardines) and wool blends.

Summertime suit fabrics include lightweight wool gabardine, linen or linen looks, rayon weaves, raw silk, silk linen, and polyester blends. You will note that almost all summertime suit fabrics have some degree of texture, from very nubby to crisper linen textures.

Fabrics most suitable for wintertime dresses include wools (knits or weaves, such as gabardine crepes or challis) and blends. These provide good choices for daywear or business looks. For evenings and holidays, velvet, taffeta, chiffon, satin, or brocade are good alternatives.

Fabrics most suitable for summertime dresses are the cottons, such as chambray, gauze, denim, broadcloth, (polished) sateen, knit, jacquard, eyelet, or lace. Rayon challis, faille, and crepe are among some of the dressier fabrics along with silk. For evening, chiffon, lace, eyelet, or polished cotton are good choices.

When preparing to purchase any garment, ask yourself the following questions:

- Is the fabric casual or dressy?

- Does the garment fabric present a quality image?

- Does this fabric destroy the richness of its companion garment?

- Are there too many textures or patterns among the garments to make them well mated?

- Does it look right? (If not, then it probably is not. WHEN IN DOUBT, DON'T!)

- Is this garment/fabric suitable for my needs?

- Can it be worn for several different occasions?

- Will this fabric wear well?

- Does this fabric wrinkle easily? Do I care?

- Will the fabric texture in the garment work with other garments in my wardrobe?

ACCESSORY FABRIC AND CLOTHES

Whenever you choose to use accessories made of fabric, compatibility is important. Some of the rules of past decades no longer apply to accessorizing your clothes today. For example, satin shoes were considered to be for eveningwear and wedding parties only. Now, they are being shown for daywear in spring and summer. Sequin and rhinestone-trimmed garments used to be appropriate for eveningwear only; now we wear them for fun, casual/chic clothes during the day.

The general principles of daywear/business clothing have not changed much, however. For instance, silk scarves are dressy and belong with this look. The dressier challis scarves are also compatible with dressy daywear garments. Casual cottons or rayon scarves belong with casual cottons and rayon garments.

Canvas shoes belong with casual cotton weaves or knits, not dressy clothes. The same is true with any other casual fabric shoe.

FIBERS

At this point in our discussion of fabric, it is important to understand some of the characteristics of natural versus synthetic fabrics. With today's technology we have options never before realized. For example, there was a time when rayon was looked upon as a second-rate fabric because it wrinkled if you sneezed. Now we have crease-resistant rayons that look just like sueded silks, wool gabardines, or silk knits that are actually found in higher-end, higher-priced clothing. We need to become more educated as consumers. Therefore you must realize the advantages of combining the best features of any fabric, natural or synthetic. Compare the assets and the liabilities of each fabric category.

■ natural fibers (cotton, wool, silk, linen)

assets	liabilities
absorb moisture nicely	dry slowly
are long-wearing	soil easily
mold nicely into desired design; tailor beautifully	will shrink if not properly laundered or cleaned
feel elegant	cannot be permanent pressed by heat setting
can be altered (seams let out) without noticeable changes or pinholes	

■ synthetic fibers

assets	liabilities
blend well with natural fibers	stain easily
do not shrink	feel clammy in hot weather and cold in winter weather because they don't breathe or allow air circulation
require little or no pressing	collect static electricity
can be permanently pleated	lack durability
cost less	susceptible to grease stains
resist wrinkles	generally do not dye well in clear, bright, intense colors
	usually retain perspiration odors

Note: Rayon is not a natural fiber, but it has some qualities of a natural fiber, such as breathability and comfort. Derived from a cellulose fiber, it does not have a chemical base.

FABRIC DEFINITIONS

Broadcloth: A lightweight plain weave, tightly woven in a thin yarn. As a cotton blend, it has a lustrous surface. Cotton or silk broadcloth is great for blouses and dresses.

Challis: A fine, lightweight fabric in smooth, firm weave. Challis is usually printed with a floral or paisley pattern. It drapes well for dresses, skirts, and scarves.

Chambray: A lightweight weave of colored and white yarns for a cool look. Sometimes referred to as lightweight denim.

Charmeuse: A medium-weight satin fabric with high luster. It has a soft draping quality. Charmeuse is good for blouses and some dresses for dressy daywear.

Cotton sheeting: This tightly woven, lightweight fabric has all the best qualities of cotton (coolness, crispness, breathability) and is also particularly durable.

Crepe: A soft, drapey fabric characterized by a slightly pebbly texture. Lighter weight is used for dresses, medium weight is used for dressy separates. Crepes may be silk, wool, or rayon.

Crêpe de chine: A very soft, lightweight fabric with a surface sheen and a silky feel. It creates a dressy look for blouses and dresses.

Denim: This rugged, durable fabric is no longer limited to the traditional indigo blue. The heavier the weight, the more durable the fabric. Basically for casualwear. It is a timeless fabric.

Faille: A semilustrous fabric with ribbed texture and excellent draping qualities. It creates a dressy look for dresses and pants/coat ensembles or separates.

Flannel: A fabric with a soft, plain or twill weave and a slightly napped surface in wool or cotton. In wool, it is best for jackets, slacks, and other sportswear. In cotton, it is best for pajamas or nightgowns.

Gauze: This thin, sheer loose weave is one of the coolest, lightest fabrics around. It is good for casual/chic separates or dresses.

Georgette: A sheer fabric; it is soft and fluid and feels slightly crepey to the touch. It is good for dressy wear.

Intarsia knit: A colored design knit into a solid background. It is usually found in sweaters.

Interlock knit: A smooth, firm knit with the same texture on both sides of the fabric, although jacquard patterns are sometimes printed. It may be cotton, rayon, or silk.

Jacquard: A method of weaving or knitting patterns right into the fabric, although occasionally they are printed. It may be cotton, rayon, or silk.

Jersey knit: A fluid, smooth-textured knit in a plain stitch. It may be cotton, silk, or a synthetic like acrylic.

Laundered cotton: A fabric that has been washed at the manufacturing stage so that it is very soft and looks unironed. It is meant to stay that way, so ironing is unnecessary. It should be worn for casualwear.

Linen-look: This crisp, plain-weave fabric has a slubbed, slightly coarse texture. It looks like natural linen but without the wrinkles. It creates dressy daywear or casual/chic separates.

Oxford cloth: A lightweight, soft fabric made in a small basketweave with a smooth surface and a very "breathable" quality. It is used primarily as a blouse or shirt fabric.

Pique: Small, raised geometric designs give this medium-weight fabric extra crispness and body. It is used for dressy daywear.

Polished cotton: A cotton-type fabric with a glazed finish that adds smoothness, stiffness, and luster. It creates daywear and summer evening looks.

Poplin: A very fine rib weave distinguishes this hard-wearing, medium-weight fabric. It is tightly woven and is used for shirts, slacks, and dresses.

Ramie: A natural fiber that looks and feels very similar to linen. Lustrous and absorbent, it is usually blended with cotton for extra softness. It creates casual/chic or daywear looks.

Rayon: This lustrous, soft yarn is found blended with many other fibers, or alone in a smooth light-weight weave. It creates casual/chic or dressy daywear looks.

Seersucker: This lightweight warm-weather fabric alternates smooth and puckered stripes for a crinkled effect and offers true no-iron ease. It creates casual or daywear looks.

Sweater knit: Generally, a heavier weight than other knits. The texture can be flat, cabled, ribbed, pebbled, etc.

Tissue faille: Similar to "faille" but smoother, lighter, and silkier. It is used for dressy daywear looks.

Viyella: A blend of 55% wool and 45% cotton. It is wonderful for shirts, skirts, and dresses.

NOTES

NOTES

CHAPTER SEVEN

AM I READY TO GO SHOPPING?

*I*f you have lots of clothes but never a thing to wear, then this chapter will help you.

A successful image is based on many individual components. There are six key actions in organizing yourself before you shop for a more "all together you."

DE-JUNKING YOUR CLOSET

When it comes to shopping, the first key action is to keep DISCIPLINED. A successful image and discipline go hand in hand. Discipline means staying true to your:

- color palette (the best colors for you),

- lifestyle (choosing clothing that best suits your lifestyle),

- body type (correct lines for your figure),

- clothing personality (your personal style), and

- budget.

The second key action is to take a physical inventory of your existing wardrobe. It starts with truly being HONEST with yourself.

- Does it still fit well? (We may not have gained a lot of weight over the past few years, but our body weight does shift as we age.)

- Have I worn it during the last year?

- Is it in my color palette?

- Is it in style as to line, color, and fabric?

Just remember, the average woman wears 20 percent of her wardrobe 80 percent of the time. What are you doing with the other 80 percent?

Try on any garment in question. If it has excellent fit, style, and quality and if you have been using it as a key part of your wardrobe, but the color is wrong, look for a good accent color in your seasonal palette which compliments and extends the usefulness of the piece—for example, a camel suit (wrong color) accented with a purple blouse and purple accessories (right color). Just remember, never spend good money on a bad investment. In other words, if you had to buy accessories in a wrong color to make the camel suit complete as an outfit, then it is time to pass the garment along. Be sure your clothing dollars take you as far as possible in what they will buy.

The third key action is to choose the three dominant colors that will coordinate with each other. These are known as your "base colors" upon which you can build your wardrobe. Dominant colors for Winter might be red, white, and black. Dominant colors for Winter II might be taupe, navy, and hunter green. Dominant colors for Summer might be gray, pink, and gardenia white. Dominant colors for Spring might be camel, ivory, and coral. Dominant colors for Autumn might be forest green, mustard yellow, and tomato red.

These base colors are used for the key basic garments we work our wardrobe around—suits, coats, jackets, skirts, or pants. These key basic garments provide the foundation upon which you build your wardrobe. Your base dominant colors can gradually increase from three

to six. Anything more than six base colors begins to defeat the purpose.

After you establish your three base colors, you can then choose your secondary colors or accent colors. Often you will be surprised as to how much you may already have in your wardrobe that meets the above criteria. We often overlook the obvious because of the clutter. Now is the time to "de-junk" your life. Eliminate the closet confusion. Get your closet down to the garments you really want.

The fourth key action is to evaluate the style of your clothing. Consistency is the secret to a good image. For example, do you have garments hanging in your closet that have hardly been worn because they just never seem to suit the occasions of your life? Do you have a hodge-podge of styles and only a few garments you really feel good in? Place your focus on a garment you like and feel good in and start building from that point.

The clothes that are creating the clutter are often hard for some people to eliminate for a variety of reasons—sentimental value, good quality, "just as soon as I lose weight," and even the memory of how hard it was to earn the money to pay for them. Whatever the reason might be for not wanting to part with an item, the important thing is to remove them from our functioning closet.

Now you are ready to organize your workable wardrobe.

The fifth key action is to put your clothes in a functional order. This means that spring/summer clothes are stored separately from fall/winter clothes. Twelve-month items remain year-round. Arrange like items together—all jackets together as well as skirts, blouses, dresses, etc. This will provide a greater visualization of your clothing potential.

The final key action is to make a list of the items that you need to purchase to extend and update your seasonal wardrobe. This should include shoes, handbags, and other accessories.

LET'S GO SHOPPING! ■

Now we are ready to go! Let's discuss the Do's and Don'ts.

DO—

■ Go shopping with a positive mental attitude. Start by focusing on all the things you like about yourself by putting your focus on looking the very best you can with your existing resources.

■ Focus your attention on specific stores or departments within stores based on your style, color palette, and budget. If you walk into a department store with no direction in mind, it is easy to become overwhelmed by the "ocean of options." What all too frequently happens in these situations is we walk in and walk out without buying anything we like. Over the years, I have heard most of my clients say, "I've looked in this store before and I never saw any of the things you have brought to me." The only difference between my shopping techniques and those of my clients is FOCUS.

■ Be sure you have purchased and have in your wardrobe your key basic garments. This is where it all starts. It may not be the most exciting part of purchasing your wardrobe, but remember the cake is the base and the frosting is what gives the cake its uniqueness.

■ Base the majority of your purchases on your key best basic garments. It is better to have five outstanding outfits and feel good and look terrific every day than to have a closet full of clothes that you do not feel comfortable in.

■ Shop for a season when stores are selling for that fashion season, even if it costs a little more. You will be paid back in the time you save.

■ Shop in coordinate separates whenever possible. This will help you develop a complete look with less time involved.

■ Buy fit, not size. In today's market, sizing consistency does not exist. It would not be unusual for you to have four sizes of clothing in your closet that appropriately fit your existing body shape.

■ Consider hiring a private wardrobe consultant if you do not have the time or do not like to shop. We recommend choosing a private individual who does not make his or her profit by the amount of clothing you buy. In other words, if he/she is affiliated with a department store, you will be limited to the resources that store provides.

■ Take advantage of sales but not necessarily to build your key wardrobe. Sales are an excellent way to add filler pieces or finishing pieces to your already established wardrobe.

■ Beware of the fabric and workmanship in a garment. A price tag is not always an indicator of quality.

■ Develop a long-range plan whenever possible that will allow you to buy your key garments at one given time for a particular season. In other words, save the $500 to purchase your look! This will accomplish several things—provide a more consistent image, save time, and save money.

■ When purchasing separates, be sure they create balance in color, line, and weight for a "total look."

■ Unbelt garments—such as coats, dresses, and jumpsuits—before trying them on; then put the belt on the garment at your natural waistline. Many times we reject a garment for the wrong reasons.

■ ■ ■ ■ ■ ■ ■ ■ ■ ■ ■ ■ ■ ■ ■

The following are the hidden destroyers of a successful image!

DON'T—

■ Buy something just because it is a good deal. This whittles away at your clothing dollars as well as your total image.

■ Piecemeal your image. A little bit here, a little bit there is a good way to find a few items to complete your look, but it's not a good way to develop your wardrobe base.

■ Spend good money on a bad investment.

■ Choose clothing that requires maintenance or skills that you don't have. For example, you cannot afford a lot of dry cleaning bills in your budget, or you do not like to iron and the garment requires pressing each time it is worn.

■ Take all the fun out of shopping by underpreparing for the event.

■ Buy the main outfit and then try to find the right shoes or accessories to complete it. Check first to see if appropriate accessories are on the market. (The different sections of the fashion industry do not always work together.)

■ Shop out of frustration. In other words, don't put your garment needs off until the last minute. When you do this, you sabotage your clothing budget and ultimately your clothing image.

■ Buy a garment if you know you do not have enough money left to complete the look. Don't buy a garment if you don't have the correct pieces to finish the look. For example, don't buy a long skirt when your full-length coat will not cover it.

■ Lock yourself into a mind-set. Finding what you like may mean adapting to what is available in the stores at a particular time.

PRINCIPLES OF PROCESS

Random shopping certainly has value. It is intended to provide us with an overview of what is current in the marketplace, who is carrying what items, prices, etc. Random shopping is also a good way to pick up accessory pieces or a "fill-in" item to extend your existing wardrobe. But if the majority of your shopping is done in this manner, then you begin to sabotage your wardrobe and sacrifice a successful image.

TIPS FOR SERIOUS SHOPPING

First of all, reduce your frustration by being prepared.

■ Be organized! This means have a goal in mind when you start out. Have your closet list, color swatches, and your samples of garments in your existing wardrobe.

■ Study the current marketplace. Develop a good sense of comparative shopping. If time permits, check the same products in different stores; prices will often vary. Keep in mind that discount stores do not always provide big savings.

■ Use the mail order resources, fashion magazines, and your local newspaper for current fashion ideas. Most newspapers publish pertinent fashion information on Thursdays and Sundays; check your local paper for publishing dates.

■ Become familiar with name brands and quality. Price is not a total indicator of quality, but it can guide us. Remember, sometimes we are paying for the designer's name and other times we get the best of both name and quality. Poor quality decisions will cost you more in the long run. Don't be fooled by a garment's affordability. You should strive to gradually upgrade the quality of your garments.

■ Know your resources and what they have to offer. Where can you get the best quality and service for the amount of money you have to spend.

HOW TO WORK WITHIN A BUDGET

Many women shop in a piecemeal manner. An article of clothing here; an item on sale there. It is much easier to justify a $50 expenditure than it is a $500 one. But all too frequently, a piecemeal approach will be one of the major destroyers of a successful image. You will best establish a clothing budget by looking over your checkbook stubs, charge slips, etc. from the previous year to determine what you have a tendency to spend on a given season's wardrobe. Often you will be amazed at how much you actually spend. When you are organizing your budget, be sure to allot dollars to finish the outfit with accessories.

Always buy the best quality you can for the amount of money you have to spend.

NOTES

CONCLUSION

*I*f you have read the various chapters in this book, you are now acquainted with the necessary aspects of developing your personal style. No secrets have been withheld! This means you now have all the needed tools to begin except one. And that one comes from within yourself… It is your attitude.

AGELESS BEAUTY

Carl Lagerfeld, designer for the House of Chanel, says "Style has nothing to do with beauty or age. It is ageless and it is an attitude of the mind." A woman who inspires others because of her look does so because of the attitude she has about herself.

If age has nothing to do with good personal style, then I believe part of the necessary attitude is ageless. A woman with this attitude never thinks of herself as growing older, only improving. She is always young at heart, growing as a person intellectually, emotionally, and spiritually. God created each of us with these attributes, and they need to be developed.

As you begin your venture to put your new found image together, remember the statement "It's a process." It does not come together overnight or in a week. You will still make mistakes, but over time they will be fewer. With each passing season, you should feel better about yourself and the choices you have made.

Review some of the sound advice contained in this book on a regular basis. This will help to keep you on track and avoid some of your past pitfalls. *Failing to plan is planning to fail.* We can no longer afford to piecemeal our wardrobe or shop haphazardly. The cost is too great!

I wish you success in your planning and fun in your shopping so that the end result will be… **All Together You!**

NOTES

ALL TOGETHER ME...
PERSONAL STYLE DEVELOPMENT CHECKLIST

SEASONAL CLASSIFICATION:

_____ Winter

_____ Winter II

_____ Summer

_____ Spring

_____ Autumn

BEST COLORS:

_____ Brights, darks, and contrasts

_____ Full range of taupes and greens

_____ All colors

_____ Pastels to brights

_____ Richer, deeper hues

HAIRSTYLE PREFERENCE:

_____ Controlled

_____ Wash and go

_____ Latest style

_____ Feminine/sexy

HAIR COLOR PREFERENCE:

_____ Natural

_____ Frosted (cool blonde)

_____ Warm highlights

_____ Cover gray

BODY TYPE/FRAME:

_____ A-Frame

_____ V-Frame

_____ H-Frame

_____ 8-Frame

_____ Combination frame

FIGURE CHALLENGES:

(e.g., short neck, heavy arms)

_____

_____

_____

_____